CW00741640

WISE SAYINGS

For Your Thoughtful Consideration

ABOUT NATURE'S LAWS, NEAR LAWS, PRINCIPLES, RULES; comprising QUOTATIONS, LEGENDS, CODES, GOSPEL, AND SUCH

(600 BC–AD 2011)

WALTER W. MOORE

authorHOUSE®

AuthorHouse™
1663 Liberty Drive
Bloomington, IN 47403
www.authorhouse.com
Phone: 1-800-839-8640

© 2011 Walter W. Moore. All rights reserved.

No part of this book may be reproduced, stored in a retrieval system, or transmitted by any means without the written permission of the author.

Published by AuthorHouse 12/28/2011

ISBN: 978-1-4678-7019-1 (hc)
ISBN: 978-1-4678-7020-7 (sc)
ISBN: 978-1-4678-7021-4 (e)

Library of Congress Control Number: 2011960703

Any people depicted in stock imagery provided by Thinkstock are models, and such images are being used for illustrative purposes only. Certain stock imagery © Thinkstock.

Because of the dynamic nature of the Internet, any web addresses or links contained in this book may have changed since publication and may no longer be valid. The views expressed in this work are solely those of the author and do not necessarily reflect the views of the publisher, and the publisher hereby disclaims any responsibility for them.

Contents

Foreword

The intent of this compilation is to educate, inspire, and amuse by thoughts expressed in the form of quotations by perceptive individuals during the last 2,500 years and to reaffirm that the way to the future is made by standing on previous concepts, as it has been always. The idea is that "There is nothing entirely new in the universe," meaning that thoughts and inventions and quotations are based in part on past knowledge, that is, by standing on the shoulders of others.

Data Sources
- my collection hobby from long ago
- various magazine and newspaper articles
- stock market advisory subscriptions
- *Investor's Business Daily*
- relatives and friends
- the Internet

Why?
In the words of Amelia Earhart, who flew across the Atlantic in a single-engine plane, "I did it because I wanted to." That's also why I selected expressions that in my judgment summarize broad concepts and have special qualities worth preserving in a readily available package.

"Sayings" Per Se
Universal laws of nature have existed since humanity came into existence. They apply to everyone who has ever existed anywhere on earth, including Adam and Eve. These laws are earthbound and cannot be broken, and they cannot be changed. They govern the universe. Most if not all natural laws have been identified. For a total perspective, there are only a few natural laws, but the essence of each concept may be expressed differently by different authors at different times and still be correct. All laws, theories, rules, quotations, doctrines, legends, codes, gospel, and such are grouped in this report under the generic term, "Wise Sayings."

In normal day-to-day living we have a cadre of common sayings that we use on the spur of the moment that spontaneously fit the occasion. One of the most popular in recent years is "OMG" for "Oh my God," which expresses a moment of surprise. "It'll all come out in the wash" if a bunch of negative things are happening. If explaining a complicated situation, we'll say that "a picture is worth a thousand words." "A piece of cake" is something that appears to be difficult but pleasurable to do. And so on, and there are far too many to enumerate. These are examples of idioms or common sayings in our normal day-to-day conversation. But idioms are not what this report is all about. Rather, it is about thoughtful statements expressed throughout the ages by people with high levels of consciousness.

Ancient Record Keeping

Some of the wise sayings in this collection go back to 600 BC, long before paper and printing preservation techniques were available. Instead, records were preserved by persons who excelled in word-for-word memory. The old Asian system of memory training was based almost entirely on the law of repetition. The secret of the Hindu system is small beginnings, gradual increases, and frequent reviews. Modern advertising uses the same techniques.

Scope

Most of the quotations are from distinguished people, such as authors, politicians, scientists, business leaders, philosophers, gurus, and others with substantial life roles. Some are from people you may know or have heard about. In total, the report includes a thousand quotations that go back as far as 2,500 years and about four hundred astute individuals. There's a lot of mental food for your thoughtful consideration. Perhaps some of the quotations will help you reach an unreachable star, if you are so inclined.

Chapter 1:
Inspirational Concepts

Miguel de Cervantes (1547–1616) was a Spanish dramatist, poet, and author whose major claim to fame was his creation of a fictional character named Don Quixote. Cervantes had a new idea about the then current way of writing. It was fiction. He created one of the greatest comic figures of world literature. The name *Don Quixote* became as famous as Sinbad, Tarzan, Odysseus, Hamlet, or Superman.

Don Quixote is considered the first modern novel and often regarded among the best works of fiction ever written. It relates the history of Don Quixote, the tall, gaunt knight-errant astride his fallible steed, a bony old barn nag he called Rocinante, with his potbellied, illiterate squire, Sancho Panza, by his side. Quixote puts on an old suit of armor which had belonged to his great grandfather and appoints himself the Knight of La Mancha. In the novel, Don Quixote dreams to become a mighty knight who travels the countryside performing good deeds and seeking adventure. Among other things, he attacks a windmill that he imagines to be a giant. He sees the windmill blades as the giant's arms. Here is what may be the most relevant portion of the novel.

> Just then they came in sight of thirty or forty windmills that rise from the plain. And no sooner did Don Quixote see them than he said to his squire, "Fortune is guiding our affairs better than we ourselves could have wished. Do you see over yonder, friend Sancho, thirty or forty hulking giants? I intend to do battle with them and slay them. With their spoils we shall begin to be rich for this is a righteous war and the removal of so foul a brood from off the face of the earth is a service God will bless."
>
> "What giants?" asked Sancho Panza.
>
> "Those you see over there," replied his master, "with their long arms. Some of them have arms well-nigh two leagues in length."
>
> "Take care, sir," cried Sancho. "Those over there are not

giants but windmills. Those things that seem to be their arms are sails which, when they are whirled around by the wind, turn the millstone."

Regardless, the mighty knight was a blundering clown who excelled at nothing but had lots of courage, good intentions, and the inspiration to pursue his dream as best he could with what he had. The *Free Merriam-Webster Dictionary* defines this quality as "Quixotic."

The words and music of a song from the musical *Man of La Mancha*, "The Impossible Dream," glorify the inspirational aspects of the Don Quixote concept. A portion of the lyrics illustrate the theme of the song:

> *To right the unrightable wrong,*
> *To try, when your arms are too weary,*
> *To reach the unreachable star ...*

> *And the world will be better for this,*
> *That one man, scorned and covered with scars,*
> *Still strove with his last ounce of courage*
> *To reach the unreachable star!*

Thus said, imagination can be a great motivator and pacifier.

(As said by Walt Disney about four hundred years later, "It's kind of fun to do the impossible.")

Quotations from Cervantes:

- The proof of the pudding is in the eating.
- The pen is the tongue of the mind.
- A proverb is a short sentence based on long experience.
- Diligence is the mother of good fortune, and idleness, its opposite, never brought a man to the goal of any of his best wishes.
- God bears with the wicked, but not forever.
- Forewarned, forearmed; to be prepared is half the victory.

• Fear has many eyes and can see things underground.

Henry David Thoreau (1817–1862) was a US author of the Transcendental movement. He is best known for Walden, *a book on simple living in natural surroundings.*

• I know of no more encouraging fact than the unquestioned ability of a man to elevate his life by conscious endeavor.
• Every man is the builder of a temple called his body.
• Men are born to succeed, not to fail.
• Our life is frittered away by detail. Simplify, simplify.

Roger Bannister (1929–) in his youth had foot-racing instincts that enabled him to smash the four-minute mile barrier that previously was considered impossible for a human. Sir Roger Gilbert Bannister became a distinguished neurologist in England.

• The man who can drive himself further once the effort gets painful is the man who will win.

Mohandas (Mahatma) Gandhi (1869–1948) became one of the most respected spiritual and political leaders of the twentieth century. He was a believer in nonviolence, but he led the campaign for Indian independence from Britain, which was achieved in 1947. India was then partitioned into India and Pakistan. Rioting between Hindus and Muslims followed.

• Strength does not come from physical capacity. It comes from indomitable will.
• You may never know what results come from your action. But if you do nothing, there will be no result.
• The greatness of a nation and its moral progress can be judged by the way its animals are treated.
• It is unwise to be too sure of one's own wisdom. It is healthy to be reminded that the strongest might weaken and the wisest might err.

Malcolm Forbes (1919–1990) was considered something of a child prodigy while growing up. His father, who founded the Forbes magazine business, was fond of saying Malcolm was loaded with sheer ability, spelled i-n-h-e-r-i-t-a-n-c-e. He enjoyed the lavish life, including his personal B-727 tri jet, and lived it up at a popular NYC nightclub every Wednesday night. He was not so lucky in politics. In a race for governor of New Jersey he was quoted as saying he was "nosed out by a landslide."

- There is never enough time, unless you are serving it.
- Keeping score of old scores and scars, getting even and one-upping, always make you less than you are.
- Ability will never catch up with the demand for it.

Michael P. Anderson *(1959–2003) was an African American who was a NASA space commander and a lieutenant colonel with the US Air Force. He was killed when the craft reentered Earth's atmosphere and disintegrated.*

- If you want something that's going to provide you with a lot of challenges and a variety of different things to do, then you really can't beat a place like the Air Force. I don't mean this to sound like a recruiting pitch. But it has been a lot of fun.

Walter Hagen *(1892–1969) was an early colorful golfer. He played in plus-four knee slacks with knee-high socks and two-toned shoes. He was the first golfer athlete named to the list of best dressed Americans. His tally of eleven major golf championships is third behind Jack Nicklaus and Tiger Woods. He was truly a dashing and assertive character and may have been the first sportsman to earn a million dollars in his career, including product fees. His first major win was in 1914 at age twenty-two. It was the 1914 US Open.*

- Don't worry. Don't hurry. You're only here for a short visit so be sure to smell the flowers along the way.
- I never wanted to be a millionaire. I just wanted to live like one.

Lee Iacocca *(1924–), you might say, was born to be busy at all times. He started when young by parking his wagon in front of grocery store* *doors and offering to haul customers' groceries to their home. He is noted for being an American industrialist and for his revival of the Chrysler Corporation in the 1980s when he was the CEO.*

- You've got to say, "I think if I keep working on this and want it bad enough, I can have it."
- Apply yourself. Get all the education you can, but then, by God, do something. Don't just stand there. Make it happen

Demosthenes *(384–322 BC) was born with a severe speech impediment. People laughed at him as a youth in ancient Athens. He practiced his elocution by talking to stones and fence posts with pebbles in his mouth. Later, Demosthenes made his living as a professional speechwriter (logographer) and a lawyer. The "Alexandrian Canon" recognized him as one of the greatest of all ancient Greek orators and logographers. Cicero acclaimed him as "the perfect orator" who lacked nothing.*

- All speech is vain and empty unless it is accompanied by action. [He made use of his body to accentuate his words and as a result was able to project his ideas and arguments more forcefully; later famous orators like Henry Clay would mimic this technique.]
- Beware lest in your anxiety to avoid war you obtain a master.
- Small opportunities are often the beginning of great enterprises.
- The easiest thing of all is to deceive one's self; for what partitioned man wishes he generally believes to be true.

Marcus Aurelius *(AD 121–180) was emperor of Rome from 161 to his death in 180 and is renowned as one of the most important Stoic philosophers.*

- Look well into thyself; there is a source which will always spring up if thou wilt always search there.

Dan Reeves *(1944–) Football coach*

- Difficulties in life are intended to make us better, not bitter.

Dale Carnegie *(1888–1955) was a strong advocate of public speaking. He became famous by teaching others how to become successful. His book on* How to Win Friends and Influence People *has sold more than 10 million copies.*

- If you can do it once, you can do it twice. If you can do twice, you can make it a habit.
- Two men looked out from prison bars. One saw the mud: the other stars.
- One of the most tragic things I know about human nature is that all of us tend to put off living. We are all dreaming of some magical rose garden over the horizon instead of enjoying the roses that are blooming outside our windows today.
- Any fool can criticize, condemn, and complain—and most fools do.

Teresa Heinz *(1938–) was married to US Senator John Heinz, who was killed in an airplane crash in 1991. He was connected to the family-owned ketchup and condiments industry. Teresa next married US Senator John Kerry, who lost the 2004 presidential election to George W. Bush. She kept the Heinz name. As she says, her legal name is Teresa Heinz, and her political name is Teresa Heinz Kerry. She is known for her extraordinary ideas and is chairman of the Heinz Endowments and Family Philanthropies. She also has twelve honorary doctoral degrees and speaks five languages.*

- Your diligence and nurturing will protect and inspire many people in your lifetime. Acknowledge, and cherish, every single quality you have, and use it, and leverage it to the fullest. Make room daily for your own time and space, so that you are able to open your door generously to others.

Duke Ellington (1899–1974) was one of the most influential figures in Big Band jazz during his time, if not in all American music.

- A problem is a chance for you to do your best.

Maxwell Maltz (1899–1975) was an American plastic surgeon and author who wrote the book Psycho-Cybernetics, *which is about communications between mind and body. It's somewhat like using "mind over matter" principles to set personal goals and make them mentally acceptable as a form of a self-help system through visualization. The thought is that one's self-image is a controlling factor on one's overall health, happiness, and success.*

- When you believe you can—you can.

Dave Thomas (1932–2002) was born to an unwed mother he never knew. He was adopted when six weeks old. He finally graduated from high school at thirty-three years of age. Thomas was the founder and chief executive officer of Wendy's, one of the top fast food restaurants specializing in hamburgers. Upon his death there were more than six thousand Wendy's restaurants. As a philanthropist, he established the Dave Thomas Foundation for Adoption.

- Don't be afraid to be unique or speak your mind, because that's what makes you different from anyone else.

Bobby Bowden (1929–) was head football coach at Florida State University. He built one of college football's greatest dynasties. He won two national championships and twelve conference championships. He was penalized twelve games for an academic scandal. His final career record was still 377 wins, 129 losses, and 4 ties.

- Anytime something goes bad, something good is going to come of it.
- I guess I'll retire someday if I live that long.

Ryszard Kapuscinski (1932–2007) was Poland's leading journalist in his time.

- Our salvation is in striving to achieve what we know we'll never achieve.

Isaac Asimov (1920–1992) was a Russian-born American author and professor of biochemistry. He wrote or edited more than five hundred books, making him one of the most prolific writers of all time. He is best known for science fiction and popular science subjects.

- The true delight is in the finding out rather than in the knowing.
- Part of the inhumanity of the computer is that, once it is competently programmed and is working smoothly, it is completely honest.
- I do not fear computers. I fear the lack of them.

G. K. Chesterton (1874–1936) was a brilliant Catholic apologist (one who defends a position or belief).

- Circumstances break men's bones; it has never been shown that they break men's optimism.
- The thing I hate about an argument is that it always interrupts a discussion.

Russell H. Conwell (1843–1925) was an American Baptist minister and an outstanding orator. He is best remembered as the founder and first president of Temple University in Philadelphia and for his lecture "Acres of Diamonds."

- Many of us spend our lives searching for success when it is usually so close that we can reach out and touch it.

Mary Tyler Moore (1936–) is a popular US television actress.

- Pain nourishes courage. You can't be brave if you've only had wonderful things happen to you.
- Take chances, make mistakes. That's how you grow. Pain nourishes your courage. You have to fail in order to practice being brave.

Norman Vincent Peale (1898–1993) is another example of a poor boy achieving success through determination. When young he helped support his family by doing odd jobs, such as delivering newspapers, working in a grocery store, and selling pots and pans door to door. He later became one of the most influential clergymen during the twentieth century. He wrote several books; the most popular, The Power of Positive Thinking, *has sold more than 20 million copies in fourteen languages.*

- People become really quite remarkable when they start thinking they can do things. When they believe in themselves, they have the first secret of success.

Denis Waitley (1924–) has written many books and delivered many keynote speeches about personal development and strategies. His theme throughout his speeches, books, and programs is the psychology of winning. His programs have sold over 10 million copies, and his life has transformed millions of lives.

- Time and health are two precious assets that we don't recognize and appreciate until they have been depleted.
- If you believe you can, you probably can. If you believe you won't, you most assuredly won't. Belief is the ignition switch that gets you off the launching pad.
- Life is the movie you see through your own eyes. It makes little difference what's happening out there. It's how you take it that counts.
- Don't dwell on what went wrong. Instead, focus your energies on moving forward toward finding the answer.
- Learn from the past, set vivid, detailed goals for the future, and live in the only moment of time over which you have any control: now.
- One characteristic of winners is they always look upon themselves as a do-it-yourself project.
- No man or woman is an island. To exist just for yourself is meaningless. You can achieve the most satisfaction when you feel related to some greater purpose in life, something greater than yourself.
- What the mind dwells upon, the body acts upon.

Thomas Edison (1847–1931) was an American inventor of Dutch origin who is considered one of the most prolific inventors in history, holding 1,093 patents in his name, as well as many patents in the United Kingdom, France, and Germany.

- I find my greatest pleasure, and so my reward, in the work that precedes what the world calls success.
- If we did all the things we are capable of, we would literally astonish ourselves.
- Discontent is the first necessity of progress.
- I have not failed. I've just found ten thousand ways it won't work.

Jeffrey Keller (1961–2010) is a speaker and writer in the area of personal development and spiritual growth. He also was an otolaryngology doctor.

- You are where you are right now in your life because of the choices you have made and the actions you have taken. If you want to change your life, remember that change starts with you.
- Motivation is like a fire; unless you add fuel, it goes out.
- Most people perform far below their potential because they are either unaware of the principles of achievement—or fail to apply them consistently. Success is not an accident—it is a learned skill.

John C Maxwell (1947–) is an American author, speaker, and leadership expert. He has written more than fifty books, which have sold more than 13 million copies, with several on the New York Times *best sellers list and translations in over fifty languages.*

- Believing in people before they have proved themselves is the key to motivating people to reach their potential.
- For most people, it's not what they are that holds them back. It's what they think they are not.
- The truth is that you can spend your life any way you want, but you can spend it only once.

William O'Neal (1933–) is an American entrepreneur, stockbroker, and writer.

- You can always learn from history because nature doesn't change and there's really not as much that's new in the market as most people seem to believe.

Bernard Baruch (1870–1965) appears to have been one born lucky in everything he touched. His medical education was financed by a distant relative. His father became famous as a chief surgeon on Robert E. Lee's staff during the Civil War. After that, he worked himself up the financial ladder and eventually bought a seat on the New York Stock Exchange. He made a fortune as stock market speculator. Later he lost his fortune but made it back several times over. After his success in business, he devoted his time toward advising Democratic presidents Woodrow Wilson and Franklin Roosevelt on economic matters. Although his remarkable achievements were made in New York and Washington, his heart was always proud of being from South Carolina. He died at age ninety-five, and it is reported that he had not lost a bit of his Southern accent. Twenty years after his death, he was inducted into the South Carolina Business Hall of Fame.

- In America, if you put your mind to it you can have anything you want. You just can't have everything you want.
- In the last analysis, our only freedom is the freedom to discipline ourselves.
- Don't try to buy at the bottom and sell at the top. It can't be done except by liars.
- Age is only a number, a cipher for the records. A man can't retire his experience. He must use it. Experience achieves more with less energy.

Alexis de Tocqueville (1805–1859) was born in Paris and became a historian specializing in politics. He was best known for his book Democracy in America.

- History is a gallery of pictures in which there are few originals and many copies.

- In politics, shared hatreds are almost always the basis of friendships.
- Consider any individual at any period of his life, and you will always find him preoccupied with fresh plans to increase his comfort.

Muriel Strode (1875–1930) was an American poet and writer. She left behind a wealth of inspiring quotations when she died. One of her best is the first one on the list below. It is so well known that people often forget the original source and quote it under the names of other writers.

- Do not follow where the path may lead. Go instead where there is no path and leave a trail.
- The smallest good deed is better than the grandest intention.
- The strength of women comes from the fact that psychology cannot explain us. Men can be analyzed, but women ... merely adored.
- If you chase two rabbits, both will escape.
- Discretion is the better part of valor.
- I like hearing myself talk. It is one of my greatest pleasures. I often have long conversations all by myself, and I am so clever that sometimes I don't understand a single word of what I am saying.
- I long to accomplish a great and noble task, but it is my chief duty to accomplish small tasks as if they were great and noble.

Julius Caesar (100–44 BC) is remembered as one of history's greatest generals and ruler of the Roman Empire. He had a love affair with Cleopatra, the ruler of Egypt, and fathered her son. It is thought that he was assassinated on March 15, a date on the Roman calendar known as "The Ides of March."

- Men in general are quick to believe that which they wish to be true.

William Arthur Ward (1921–1994) was the author of Fountains of Faith *and one of America's most quoted writers of inspirational concepts as well as an excellent motivational speaker.*

- The pessimist complains about the wind; the optimist expects it to change; the realist adjusts the sails.
- Do more than belong: participate. Do more than care: help. Do more than believe: practice. Do more than be fair: be kind. Do more than forgive: forget. Do more than dream: work. Flatter me, and I will not believe you. Criticize me, and I may not like you. Ignore me, and I may not forgive you. Encourage me, and I will not forget you. Love me, and I may be forced to love you.
- Wise are they who have learned these truths: Trouble is temporary. Time is tonic. Tribulation is a test tube.
- It is wise to direct your anger toward problems, not people; to focus your energies on answers, not excuses. We can learn much from wise words, little from wisecracks, and less from wise guys.
- Opportunity is often difficult to recognize. We usually expect it to beckon us with beepers and billboards.
- God gave you a gift of 86,400 seconds today. Have you used one to say "thank you"?

Bill Gross *(1944–), director of Pimco, is perhaps the most successful bond investor of this generation. He has been referred to as "the Warren Buffett of the bond world." Gross manages the Pimco Total Returns Fund. He began his career as a blackjack counter in Las Vegas.*

- Markets invariably move to undervalued and overvalued extremes because human nature falls victim to greed and/ or fear.

Albert Schweitzer *(1875–1965) was a man of many talents. He was not considered a child genius, but in his teens he began to develop a lot of curiosity about life and the will to live. He got a doctoral degree in philosophy and later a medical doctorate. He devoted his life to providing health care for the deprived people of equatorial Africa where living conditions were terrible. "Reverence for Life" is a concept he nurtured to express the thought that life is something we share with* *thing that lives—from elephants to blades of grass—and that all living things are like brothers and sisters. However, suffering and death are inevitable because we all want to live. So we harvest crops, eat bread made from grains, grill steaks, and kill insects. Even vegetarians must eat some living things to survive. Doctor Schweitzer was a forerunner of the great humanitarian and ecological movements of the twentieth century, including environmental and animal welfare movements. The concept spread round the world for many years and was taught in schools in almost every language in the world. Schweitzer was awarded the Nobel Peace Prize in 1953 for his philosophy of Reverence for Life. By the time of his death at age ninety, his hospital in Africa consisted of seventy-two buildings with beds for six hundred patients.*

- Sometimes our light goes out but is blown into flame by another human being. Each of us owes deepest thanks to those who have rekindled this light.

Brian Tracy *(1944–) is considered by those who know him to be a personal development and self-improvement guru. His audience has been confined to the business world and not the country at large. His style consists of talks at seminars and pass-out literature on leadership, sales management effectiveness, and business strategy. People like Brian Tracy do not make universal headlines but play a significant role in advancing the business community. His voice of experience shines through in his quotes.*

- Successful people are always looking for opportunities to help others. Unsuccessful people are always asking, "What's in it for me?"
- When you develop yourself to the point where your belief in yourself is so strong that you know you can accomplish anything you put your mind to, your future will be unlimited.
- Practice golden rule one of management in everything you do: manage others the way you would like to be managed.
- At least 80 percent of millionaires are self-made. That is, they started with nothing but ambition and energy, the same way most of us start.

- Ask for what you want. Ask for help, ask for input, ask for advice and ideas—but don't be afraid to ask.
- Throughout the developed world, we have moved from "manpower" to "mind power." We have moved from the use of physical muscle to the use of mental muscle.
- The kindest thing you can do for the people you care about is to become a happy, joyous person.
- An average person with average talent, ambition, and education can outstrip the most brilliant genius in our society, if that person has clear, focused goals.
- The history of the human race is the history of ordinary people who have overcome their fears and accomplished extraordinary things.
- To overcome fear, act as if it was impossible to fail, and it shall be.
- Manage by objectives. Tell people exactly what you want them to do, and then get out of their way.
- Manage by responsibility. It is a powerful way to grow people.
- The single common denominator of men and women who achieve great things is a sense of destiny.
- You contain within yourself a unique combination of talents and abilities which, properly identified and applied, will enable you to achieve virtually any goal you can set for yourself.
- I've found that luck is quite predictable. If you want more luck, take more chances. Be more active. Show up more often.

John Wayne (1907–1979) was idolized by many as the epitome of a rugged cowboy in Western movies. He was rated thirteenth on the list of Greatest Male Stars of All Time in 2007 by the American Film Institute. He ranked third among America's favorite film stars in a Harris Poll in 2007, and he was the only deceased star on the list. He was in over seventy-five films in total and over fifty feature films.

- Tomorrow is the most important thing in life. Comes in to us at midnight very clean. It's perfect when it arrives, and it puts itself in our hands and hopes we have learned something from yesterday.

- Courage is being scared to death ... and saddling up anyway.
- Life is tough, but it's tougher when you're stupid.
- If you've got them by the balls, their hearts and minds will follow.

Orville C. Wetmore (1919–) was a Du Pont employee and personal friend.

- The only thing you learn from history is that you don't learn anything from history.

Leonardo da Vinci (1452–1519) started life as an illegitimate son of a notary, and a peasant mother. He became what many consider to be one of the greatest painters of all time. He is also thought to be perhaps the most diversely talented person ever to have lived. His most famous portraits were Mona Lisa *and* The Last Supper. *Clues from his paintings became the basis of a detective murder mystery novel authored by Dan Brown entitled* The Da Vinci Code. *It was published in 2004 and became a worldwide best seller. It sold 80 million copies by 2009 and had been translated into forty-four languages. A part of the intrigue was that it portrayed the possibility that Mary Magdalene was one of the twelve disciples, that she was married to Jesus, and that they begat at least three children. One of the secrets revealed in the novel is that the person on Jesus's right side in the Last Supper portrait was Mary Magdalene, not the apostle John. In the novel, the absence of the apostle John is explained by da Vinci's knowledge that John is referred to as "the disciple that Jesus loved," a code name for Mary Magdalene. Also, no chalice is shown in the painting. Even today, there is a lot of conjecture on the whereabouts of the Holy Grail, commonly believed to be the cup that Jesus used. The novel says, "The Holy Grail is not a physical chalice, but a woman, namely Mary Magdalene, who carried the bloodline of Christ."*

- Water is the driving force of all nature.
- Nature never breaks her own laws.
- Simplicity is the ultimate sophistication.

- You can have no dominion greater or less than that over yourself.
- In rivers, the water that you touch is the last of what has passed and the first of that which comes; so with present time.
- Iron rusts from disuse; water loses its purity from stagnation ... even so does inaction sap the vigor of the mind.
- It has long since come to my attention that people of accomplishment rarely sit back and let things **happen** to them. They went out and happened to things.
- It's easier to resist at the beginning than at the end.
- Once you have tasted flight, you will walk the earth with your eyes turned skyward, for there you have been, and there you will long to return.

Joe Paterno (1924 -) Nittany Lions head coach since 1966. Currently he is the football coach with the most wins ever.

- Believe deep down in your heart that you're destined to do great things.
- Besides pride, loyalty, discipline, heart and mind, confidence is the key to all locks.

The Little Engine that Could. This fable was written back in a time when locomotives ran on steam engines fueled by coal or wood. The steam would make a regular sound of chugga, chugga, chugga *when traveling on level railroads. The sound was louder and slower when departing a station or pulling a heavy load and faster on downhill grades. And so it was one day when the little engine was hauling a load of toys for some children. It approached a steep hill. The* chug, chug, chug *sound slowed as it started climbing the hill. People say the engine was saying to itself, "I think I can, I think I can, I think I can," over and over. Later on as the hill got steeper the little engine was saying the words slower: "I ... think ... I ... can, I ... think ... I ... can." Then as it reached the top and started down, it said, slowly at first, "I thought I could, I thought I could." As the downhill speed increased, the people said the little train was smiling and singing, "ThotIcould, thotIcould, thotIcould," over and over until it reached the station.*

Chapter 2:
Admonitions

James Joyce (1882–1941) was an Irish novelist noted for his experimental use of language in such works as Ulysses *(1922) and* Finnegans Wake *(1939).*

- Mistakes are portals of discovery.

Baltasar Gracian (1601–1658) was a Spanish Baroque philosopher and prose writer.

- Never do anything when you are in a temper, for you will do everything wrong.
- Never contend with a man who has nothing to lose.

CHOPIN, MOZART, AND BEETHOVEN

- Learn to identify the music of Chopin, Mozart, and Beethoven.

Ludwig van Beethoven (1770–1827) is the most famous classical composer (Mozart aside) of the Western world. Bom-bom-bom bommmmmm … The opening notes of Beethoven's Symphony No. 5 in C Minor are probably the most famous fragment in all classical music.

Wolfgang Amadeus Mozart (1756–1791) is one of the heavyweights of classical music, generally placed in the top rank of composers along with Beethoven and Bach. Many consider Mozart to be the greatest composer of all time. He was a child prodigy who wrote his first symphony at age eight and then grew into a prolific adult who wrote more than six hundred published works.

Frederic Chopin (1810–1849) was a renowned child-prodigy pianist. All his works involve the piano.

Margaret Thatcher (1925–) was British prime minister from 1979 to 1990.

- The most important thing in communication is to hear what isn't being said.
- A stumble may prevent a fall.
- Being powerful is like being a lady. If you have to tell people you are, you aren't.
- If you just set out to be liked, you would be prepared to compromise on anything at any time, and you would achieve nothing.

Anonymous

- Accept your environment and adapt yourself to it in silence, instead of noisily attempting to adapt your environment to yourself.
- Measure wealth not by the things you have but by the things you have for which you would not take money.

Seneca (4 BC–AD 65) was a Roman Stoic philosopher, statesman, and dramatist. He was later advisor to Emperor Nero.

- We should every night call ourselves to an account: What infirmity have I mastered today? What passions opposed? What temptation resisted? What virtue acquired?

Dag Hammarskjöld (1905–1961) was a well-educated Swedish diplomat, economist, and writer. He became Secretary-General of the United Nations for eight years until his death in a plane crash in 1961. President John F. Kennedy called him "the greatest statesman of our century." He was the first to be awarded the Nobel Peace Prize posthumously.

- "Freedom from fear" could be said to sum up the whole philosophy of human rights.
- The assembly has witnessed over the last weeks how historical truth is established; once an allegation has been repeated a few times, it is no longer an allegation, it is an

established fact, even if no evidence has been brought out in order to support it.

• There is a point at which everything becomes simple and there is no longer any question of choice, because all you have staked will be lost if you look back. Life's point of no return.

Victor-Marie Hugo (1802–1885) was a Frenchman with many talents in the writing world, mostly as a poet and a novelist. Some thought he might be the greatest French poet. He also achieved fame for two novels, Les Misérables *and* The Hunchback of Notre-Dame.

• All the forces in the world are not as powerful as an idea whose time has come.
• A mother's arms are made of tenderness, and children sleep soundly in them.
• A man is not idle because he is absorbed in thought. There is a visible labor, and there is an invisible labor.

Mae Jemison (1956–) is a physician and a NASA astronaut and the first African American woman to travel in space.

• Failure to recognize possibilities is the most dangerous and common mistake one can make.
• A prudent person avoids unpleasant things; but a wise person overcomes them.

Sir Walter Raleigh (1552–1618) had a colorful life. He always was stirring the pot, looking for some way to stay busy either in the new world or at home in England. Some of his known activities are enumerated below:

1. *He was an English aristocrat.*
2. *He rose rapidly in the favor of Queen Elizabeth I.*
3. *He sailed on an expedition to find the "city of gold" in South America. He did not find it but wrote an exaggerated account of the expedition.*
4. *He was knighted in 1586.*

5. *He was one of the grand scalawags of the Elizabethan age.*
6. *He created a legend that he once laid his cloak on a mud puddle for the Queen so she would not get mud all over her shoes.*
7. *He was well known for popularizing tobacco in England.*
8. *He was involved in the colonization of Virginia.*
9. *He secretly married one of Queen Elizabeth's ladies-in-waiting without the Queen's permission, for which he and his wife were imprisoned in the Tower of London.*
10. *After Queen Elizabeth died in 1603, Raleigh was again imprisoned in the Tower for allegedly being involved in the Main Plot against King James I.*
11. *He was released to conduct a second expedition to find the "city of gold." This also was unsuccessful, but men under his command ransacked a Spanish outpost.*
12. *He returned to England. Spain was upset about the outpost ransacking, and to appease them, Raleigh was beheaded in 1618.*

Voltaire (1694–1778) was one of France's greatest writers and philosophers.

- Judge others by their questions rather than by their answers.
- Do the hard jobs first. The easy jobs will take care of themselves.
- If God did not exist, it would be necessary to invent him.
- Anything too stupid to be said is sung.
- Every man is guilty of all the good he didn't do.
- ... the safest course is to do nothing against one's conscience. With this secret, we can enjoy life and have no fear from death.
- To succeed in the world it is not enough to be stupid, you must also be well-mannered.

Zig Ziglar (1926–) came from humble early life in Alabama and Mississippi. He was the tenth of twelve children. He became a self-help motivational speaker and an author. Ten of his twenty-five books have been best sellers.

- You cannot tailor-make the situations in life, but you can tailor-make the attitudes to fit those situations.
- Money isn't the most important thing in life, but it's reasonably close to oxygen on the "gotta have it" scale.
- God's way is still the best way.
- A lot of people quit looking for work as soon as they find a job.
- Every choice you make has an end result.
- If you treat your wife like a thoroughbred, you'll never end up with a nag.
- Every obnoxious act is a cry for help.
- Many marriages would be better if the husband and the wife clearly understood that they are on the same side.

Aldous Huxley (1894–1963) was an English writer and one of the most prominent of the famous Huxley family. By the end of his life, Huxley was considered, in some academic circles, a leader of modern thought and an intellectual of the highest rank.

- Happiness is not achieved by the conscious pursuit of happiness; it is generally the by-product of other activities.

Norman Schwarzkopf (1934–), also known as Stormin' Norman, retired US Army four-star general, was commander of the coalition forces in the Gulf War of 1991.

- Your organization will never get better unless you are willing to admit that there is something wrong with it.
- [A journalist asked if there was room for forgiveness toward the people who abetted the 9/11 terrorist attacks against America.] I believe that forgiving them is God's function. Our job is simply to arrange the meeting.

Jim Rohn (1930–2009) became famous for his motivational speeches and video programs. He often used four motivational questions: Why?

Why not? Why not you? *and* Why not now? *He was a best-selling author of many training programs, such as "The Art of Exceptional Living" and "The Power of Ambition" Many considered him to be one of the most influential thinkers of our time.*

- Learn to express rather than impress. Expressing evokes a me-too attitude, while impressing evokes a so-what attitude.
- When you know what you want, and want it bad enough, you will find a way to get it.
- Without a sense of urgency, desire loses its value.
- You must constantly ask yourself these questions: Who am I around? What are they doing to me? What have they got me reading? What have they got me saying? Where do they have me going? What do they have me thinking? And most important, what do they have me becoming? Then ask yourself the big question: Is that okay? Your life does not get better by chance, it get better by change.
- There is a very thin line between faith and folly. Affirmations without action can be the beginning of self-delusion. And for your well-being, there is little worse than self-delusion.
- The key is to take a step today. Whatever the project, start today. Start clearing out a drawer of your newly organized desk—today. Start setting your first goal—today. Start listening to motivational programs—today. Start a sensible weight-reduction plan—today.

Veterans of Foreign Wars (VFW) *is an organization composed of combat and supporting military personnel who were sent overseas.*

- It's not the price you pay to be a member; it's the price you paid to become eligible.

Michelangelo Buonarroti *(1475–1564) was one of the greatest sculptors, architects, and painters of the Italian Renaissance period. His reputation is still well known today. Many of his sculptures, buildings, and paintings are still around today, but he didn't leave many widely known quotations.*

- The greatest danger for most of us is not that our aim is too high and we miss, but that it is too low and we achieve it.

Paul A. Fine (1935–) is an industrial psychologist, market research consultant, and personal friend of the author.

- The power of inanimate objects to defy the will of man is directly proportional to the urgency of the moment. I.e., shoestrings break at the wrong time, traffic lights turn red when you are rushed for time, and toast falls buttered side down. (Five green lights in a row is a sign you are in tune with the elements.)

Laozi, also spelled Lao Tzu, thought to have lived between 600 BC and 200 BC, was a philosopher of ancient China and an important figure in the origin of Taoism. According to Chinese tradition, Laozi lived in the sixth century BC.

- In this world, there is nothing softer or thinner than water. But to compel the hard and unyielding, it has no equal. That the weak overcomes the strong, that the hard gives way to the gentle—this everyone knows. Yet no one asks accordingly.

William Shakespeare (1564–1616) was an English poet and playwright, widely regarded as the greatest writer in the English language and the world's preeminent dramatist. He wrote 38 plays, 154 sonnets, 2 long narrative poems, and several other poems that still survive. His plays have been translated into every major language.

- This above all: to thine own self be true; and it must follow, as the night the day, thou canst not then be false to any man. (*Hamlet*)
- Be not afraid of greatness: some men are born great, some achieve greatness and some have greatness thrust upon them. (*Twelfth Night*)
- All the world's a stage, and all the men and women merely players: they have their exits and their entrances; and one

man in his time plays many parts, his acts being seven stages. (*As You Like It*)

- The devil can cite scripture for his purpose. (*Merchant of Venice*, Act I scene 3)

Virgil (70–19 BC) was a poet who authored the Roman Empire's national epic.

- Do not trust the horse, Trojans! Whatever it is, I fear the Greeks, even though they bring gifts.

Salvador Dalí (1904–1989) was a Spanish painter who wrote three autobiographies. An independent biographer says he was one of the most brilliant artists known to mankind. Another says he was without a doubt a genius.

- At the age of six, I wanted to be a cook. At seven, I wanted to be Napoleon. And my ambition has been growing steadily ever since.
- Each morning when I awake, I experience again a supreme pleasure—that of being Salvador Dalí.
- Have no fear of perfection—you'll never reach it.

Harriet Beryl Barkier (1858–1913) was a psychologist.

- Striving for excellence motivates you. Striving for perfection is demoralizing.

Pablo Picasso (1881–1973) was a Spanish artist who made a tremendous fortune during his ninety-one years of life. His paintings were known worldwide and sold for multiple millions of dollars. For one, his portrait of his lover Dora Maar sold for $95 million. Another measure of his talent is that his paintings were high on the most stolen list. Picasso most certainly was one of the best-known characters in twentieth-century art.

- The world today doesn't make sense, so why should I paint pictures that do?

- Everyone wants to understand paintings. Why is there no attempt to understand the song of birds?
- All children are artists. The problem is how to remain an artist once he grows up.
- Bad artists copy. Good artists steal.
- Computers are useless. They can only give you answers.

A sign on the wall at the Daytona Beach Veterans Administration Day Clinic.

- The price of freedom is visible here.

Samuel Truett Cathy (1921–) is the founder and chairman of the Chick-Fil-A quick-service restaurant. His privately held company has grown to 1,300 restaurants in thirty-seven states and has thirty-nine consecutive years of annual sales growth. Revenue in 2007 was $2.74 billion.

- Take advantage of "unexpected opportunities".
- It's better to build boys than mend men.

Sir Winston Churchill (1874–1965) was a British politician and statesman known for his leadership of the United Kingdom during the Second World War. He was widely regarded as one of the great wartime leaders. He served as Prime Minister from 1940 to 1945 and again from 1951 to 1955.

- Prisoner of war! ....You are in the power of your enemy. You must obey his orders, go where he tells you, stay where you are bid, await his pleasure, and possess your soul in patience.
- A man does what he must—in spite of personal consequences, in spite of obstacles and dangers and pressures—and that is the basis of all human morality. [Note: About the same as "A man's gotta do what a man's gotta do."]
- The inherent vice of capitalism is the unequal sharing of the blessing. The inherent blessing of socialism is the equal sharing of misery.

- I contend that for a nation to try to tax itself into prosperity is like a man standing in a bucket and trying to lift himself up by the handle..

Samuel Moore Walton (1918–1992) had an idea, nurtured it into the world's largest retail organization, and became the richest man in the world. He grew up during the Great Depression and learned the value of money and hard work from a poor boy's viewpoint. His vision was about a discount department/variety store. His family became involved, and they are one of the wealthiest families of the world. The first Wal-Mart store opened in 1962 and was listed on the New York Stock Exchange in1969. Their stock was priced at about $5 per share in current dollars. It is now $56, and there have been at least two 2-for-1 stock splits. Total sales volume in 2010 was $419 billion, and their earnings were $15.6 billion. This includes a contingent warehouse concept named Sam's Club that opened in 1983. (Note: A billion is one thousand million.)

- Capital isn't scarce; vision is.
- High expectations are the key to everything.
- I had to pick myself up and get on with it, do it all over again, only better this time.
- I probably have traveled and walked into more variety stores than anybody in America. I am just trying to get ideas, any kind of ideas that will help our company. Most of us don't invent ideas. We take the best ideas from someone else.
- There is a lot more business out there in small-town America than I ever dreamed of.

Michael Gartner (1938–), former president of NBC News, has been an editor of newspapers large and small.

- Believe everything happens for a reason.
- If you get a chance, take it, and if it changes your life, let it.
- Nobody said life would be easy. They just promised it would most likely be worth it.

- Life is too short to wake up with regrets. So love people who treat you right. Forget about the ones who don't.
- Enjoy life now—it has an expiration date!

Palm Coast Newsletter, August 2010

- The time you enjoy wasting is not wasted time.

Helen Keller *(1880–1968) was an American author, political activist, and lecturer. She was the first deaf and blind person to earn a bachelor of arts degree.*

- I am only one, but still I am one. I cannot do everything; but still I can do something; and because I cannot do everything, I will not refuse to do something that I can do.

Socrates *(469–399 BC) was one of the great Greek philosophers.*

- Enjoy yourself—it's later than you think.
- Once made equal to man, woman becomes his superior.
- The beginning of wisdom is a definition of terms.
- By all means marry. If you get a good wife, you will become happy, and if you get a bad one, you will become a philosopher.
- Our prayers should be for blessings in general, for God knows what is good for us.
- Contentment is natural wealth; luxury is artificial poverty.

Walt Disney *(1901–1966) was an American film producer, director, screenwriter, voice actor, animator, entrepreneur, entertainer, international icon, and philanthropist. He and brother Roy created a number of the world's most famous fictional characters, including Mickey Mouse. The Walt Disney Company, with revenues of approximately $35 billion, has resorts in California, Florida, Japan, France, and China.*

- It's kind of fun to do the impossible.

- If you can dream it, you can do it.
- Crowded classrooms and half-day sessions are a tragic waste of our greatest national resource—the minds of our children.
- Laughter is America's most important export.
- When you are curious, you find lots of interesting things to do.
- There is more treasure in books than in all the pirates' loot on Treasure Island.
- There is nothing funnier than the human animal.
- You may not realize it when it happens, but a kick in the teeth may be the best thing in the world for you.
- Of all of our inventions for mass communication, pictures still speak the most universally understood language.
- The way to get started is to quit talking and begin doing.
- Disneyland will never be completed. It will continue to grow as long as there is imagination left in the world.
- Disneyland is the star; everything else is in the supporting role.
- Animation offers a medium of storytelling and visual entertainment which can bring pleasure and information to people of all ages everywhere in the world.
- You're dead if you only aim for kids. Adults are only kids grown up, anyway.
- I only hope that we don't lose sight of one thing—that it was all started by a mouse.
- When people laugh at Mickey Mouse, it's because he's so human.

H. Jackson Brown Jr (1948–) is an American author best known for his book Life's Little Instruction Book, *which was a* New York Times *best seller.*

- Nothing is more expensive than a missed opportunity.
- Our character is what we do when we think no one is looking.
- Sometimes the heart sees what is invisible to the eye.
- In the confrontation between the stream and the rock,

the stream always wins—not through strength but by perseverance.

- Let the refining and improving of your own life keep you so busy that you have little time to criticize others.
- If your life is free of failures, you're not taking enough risks.
- Always kiss your children good night, even if they are already asleep.
- Choose your life's mate carefully. From this one decision will come 90 percent of all your happiness or misery.
- Good manners sometimes means simply putting up with other people's bad manners.
- Life doesn't require that we be the best, only that we try our best.
- Live so that when your children think of fairness, caring, and integrity, they think of you.
- Love is when the other person's happiness is more important than your own.

Tennessee Williams (1911–1983) was a major American playwright of the twentieth century.

- Success is blocked by concentrating on it and planning for it … Success is shy—it won't come out while you are watching.

Officer Review Magazine, November 2007, page 12:

- In the early years of the last century, the philosopher George Santayana famously observed, those who cannot remember the past are condemned to repeat it. The same idea has been expressed in similar words and in earlier ages by such men as Euripides and Thucydides

Euripides (ca. 480 BC–406 BC) was a dramatist and one of the great philosophers. Little is known about Euripides, and most recorded sources are based on legend and hearsay. Ancient scholars thought that Euripides had written ninety-five plays.

- In this world second thoughts, it seems, are best.

- Never say that marriage has more of joy than pain.
- Man's best possession is a sympathetic wife.
- Talk sense to a fool, and he calls you foolish.
- The best and safest thing is to keep a balance in your life, acknowledge the great powers around us and in us. If you can do that and live that way, you are a wise man.
- Your very silence shows you agree.
- A sweet thing, for whatever time, to visit in dreams the dear father we have lost.
- Slight not what's near, while aiming at what's far.

Sophocles *(ca. 496–406 BC) was one of the great Greek dramatists and philosophers.*

- Chance never helps those who do not help themselves.
- Reason is God's greatest gift to man.
- One word frees us from all the weight and pain of life: That word is love.
- All mortal lives are set in danger and perplexity: one day to prosper, and the next—who knows?
- When all is well, then look for rocks ahead.
- A man can get a reputation from very small things.
- Kindness begets kindness evermore.
- Time eases all things.
- No wound is worse than counterfeited love.
- Unwanted favors gain no gratitude.
- Nothing abides; the starry night, our wealth, our sorrows pass away.
- The long unmeasured pulse of time moves everything.
- To find yourself, think for yourself.
- Employ your time in improving yourself by other men's writings so that you shall come easily by what others have labored hard for.

Max Born *(1882–1970) was a German physicist who won the Nobel Prize for physics in 1954.*

- The belief that there is only one truth, and that oneself is in possession of it, is the root of all evil in the world.

Chapter 3:
Religiously Speaking

God

- With me, all things are possible.

Jesus Christ (7–2 BC to AD 26–36). The incarnate Son of God and the Redeemer of the human race.

- All things, therefore, that you want men to do to you, you also must likewise do to them. [The Golden Rule, Matthew 7:12]

Ravi Jans is an Indian who is one of my personal guiding angels.

- Look forward.

Street Gospel

- God helps those who help themselves
- Everybody should believe in something. (I believe I'll have another beer.)
- The mistakes we aren't allowed to make in our youth, we make later on in life—at greater cost and with less benefit.
- Don't sweat the small stuff.
- Never use such expressions as "I can't afford it" or "I can't do this." Your subconscious mind takes you at your word.

Marianne Williamson (1952–) is a spiritual activist, author, lecturer, and founder of The Peace Alliance. She is a grassroots campaigner supporting legislation currently before Congress to establish a US Department of Peace.

- The practice of forgiveness is our most important

33

contribution to the healing of the world. Our deepest fear is not that we are inadequate. Our deepest fear is that we are powerful beyond measure.

Francis Spellman (1889–1967) served as Archbishop of New York from 1939 until his death and was named a cardinal by Pope Pius XII in 1946.

- Pray as if everything depended upon God, and work as if everything depended upon man.

Morrie Schwartz (1916–1995) wanted to be "a teacher to the last." In preparation, he got his Masters and PhD from the University of Chicago and taught sociology at Brandies University for many years. He continued to teach after he was diagnosed with ALS at the age of seventy-six. His new classes incorporated what he was learning about—the meaning of life—as he faced impending death. During this period he was interviewed by Ted Koppel, a TV news communicator on Nightline. *A former student, Mitch Albom, saw the TV show and began visiting Morrie every Tuesday. The interviews were shown on TV as* Tuesdays with Morrie. *Sadly, Morrie died within a week of the last episode, thus fulfilling a desire to teach to the last. Mitch Albom wrote a best-selling book,* Tuesdays with Morrie, *which was published in 1997 and later made into a movie.*

- Death ends a life, not a relationship.
- Everything that gets born dies.
- One hundred and ten years from now no one who is here now will be alive.
- So many people walk around with a meaningless life. They seem half-asleep, even when they're busy doing things they think are important. This is because they're chasing the wrong things.
- It's not too late to … ask yourself if you really are the person you want to be, and if not, who do you want to be.

Mitch Albom (1958–) is a US novelist and newspaper columnist for the Detroit Free Press. *He worked with Morrie Schwartz on a weekly*

TV show known as Tuesdays with Morrie. *He also published a book by the same title.*

- Holding anger is a poison. It eats you from the inside. We think that hating is a weapon that attacks the person who harmed us. But hatred is a curved blade. And the harms we do, we do to ourselves.

Oliver Wendell Holmes Sr *(1809–1894) was a physician by profession but achieved fame as a writer. He was one of the best-regarded American poets of the nineteenth century.*

- You commit a sin of omission if you do not utilize all the power that is within you.

Nick Zaharis *(1921–) is a personal friend and a Greek who thinks like Aristotle.*

- Religion is in its infancy.

Plotinus *(ca. AD 205–270) was a major philosopher of the ancient world who is widely considered the founder of Neoplatonism.*

- We are not separate from spirit, we are in it.

Anonymous Prayer

- God, grant me the serenity to accept the things I cannot change, courage to change the things I can, and wisdom to know the difference.

Pierre Teilhard de Chardin *(1881–1955) was a visionary French Jesuit, paleontologist, and philosopher who spent the bulk of his life trying to integrate religious experience with natural science, most specifically Christian theology with theories of evolution. In this endeavor Teilhard became absolutely enthralled with the possibilities for humankind, which he saw as heading for an exciting convergence of systems, an "Omega point" where the coalescence of consciousness will lead us to a new state of peace and planetary unity. He saw this unity as being* *based intrinsically upon the spirit of the Earth. Yet Teilhard's writings clearly reflect the sense of the Earth as having its own autonomous personality and being the prime center and director of our future—a strange attractor if you will—that will be the guiding force for the synthesis of humankind. The only truly natural and real human unity is the spirit of the Earth. The sense of Earth is the irresistible pressure which will come at the right moment to unite humankind in a common passion.*

- We are not human beings having a spiritual experience. We are spiritual beings having a human experience.
- The age of nations is past. The task before us now, if we would not perish, is to build the Earth.
- We have reached a crossroads in human evolution where the only road which leads forward is toward a common passion ... To continue to place our hopes in a social order achieved by external violence would simply amount to our giving up all hope of carrying the Spirit of the Earth to its limits.
- In the final analysis, the question of why bad things happen to good people transmutes itself into some very different questions, no longer asking why something happened but asking how we will respond, what we intend to do now that it happened.

Benjamin Disraeli *(1804–1881) was British Prime Minister in 1868 and 1874–1880.*

- One of the hardest things in this world is to admit you are wrong. And nothing is more helpful in resolving a situation than its frank admission.

Aesop *(620–560 BC), a Greek slave, compiled fables that have become universally known.*

- No act of kindness, no matter how small, is ever wasted.
- We hang the petty thieves and appoint the great ones to public office.

Bible

- It is more blessed to give than to receive. (Acts 20:35)
- For the love of money is the root of all evil: which while some coveted after, they have erred from the faith, and pierced themselves through with many sorrows. (1 Timothy 6:10)
- Be sober, be vigilant; because your adversary the devil, as a roaring lion, walketh about, seeking whom he may devour. (1 Peter 5:8)

Brother Bear is a 2003 animated film produced by Walt Disney.

- I think there are two types of prayer, that which is ritualistic and that which we do daily. Ritualistic prayer is used for ceremonies; daily prayer is more like a conversation with our grandfather.

Diana Robison (?)

- Prayer is when you talk to God; meditation is when you listen to God.

Harry Emerson Fosdick (1878–1969) was ordained a Baptist minister in 1903 and became pastor of the Park Avenue Baptist Church, New York City, in 1930.

- God is not a cosmic bellboy for whom we can press a button to get things done.
- God understands our prayers even when we can't find the words to say them.

Meg Wheatley (?) is an internationally acclaimed speaker, writer, and management consultant.

- Probably the most visible example of unintended consequences ... without reflection, we go blindly on our way, creating more unintended consequences.
- Destroying is a necessary function in life. Everything has

its season, and all things eventually lose their effectiveness and die.

William James (1842–1910) was a US-born psychologist and philosopher.

- Acceptance of what has happened is the first step to overcoming the consequences of any misfortune.

O. A. Battista (1917–1995) was a Canadian-American chemist and author and a devout Catholic. He was notable in his writing for not shying away from advertising his religious beliefs as well as his scientific ones.

- Some of God's greatest gifts are unanswered prayers.
- One of the most lasting pleasures you can experience is the feeling that comes over you when you genuinely forgive an enemy—whether he knows it or not.
- The greatest weakness of most humans is their hesitancy to tell others how much they love them while they are still alive.
- God gives every bird its food, but He does not throw it in the nest.
- The best eraser in the world is a good night's sleep.
- A happy marriage is the world's best bargain.
- One of the hardest things to teach a child is that the truth is more important than the consequences
- Success is getting what you want, but happiness is wanting what you've got.
- A grudge is a heavy thing to carry. It's over, let it go.
- Temptations, unlike opportunities, will always give you many second chances.
- You have reached the pinnacle of success as soon as you become uninterested in money, compliments, or publicity.

Reinhold Niebuhr (1892–1971) was an American theologian, teacher, and communicator.

- All human sin seems so much worse in its consequences than in its intentions.

Muriel Strode (1875–1930) was an American poet and writer. She left behind an abundance of inspiring quotations when she died. One of her best is the first one on the list below. It is so well known that people often forget the original source and quote it under the names of other writers.

- Practicing the Golden Rule is not a sacrifice; it is an investment.
- Religion is for those who don't want to go to hell. Spirituality is for those of us who have already been through it.

Ron Reid (1924–) is a parapsychologist and exorcist. He has had many encounters with ghosts. As a hypnotist, he can regress people's minds to lives they have lived before. He also is a proponent of meditation exercises.

- I encountered a ghost one night while exorcizing a house. I was sitting on a window ledge, and it literally pushed me out the window.
- Saying "C A L M M M M" slowly restores calmness. Tongue on top of mouth restores calmness.

Mother Teresa (1910–1970) felt strongly the call of God at the age of twelve. Her work has been recognized throughout the world. Her full name was Agnes Gonxha Bojaxhiu, She became a Catholic nun who founded the Missionaries of Charity in Calcutta, India.

- We shall never know all the good that a simple smile can do.
- We ourselves feel that what we are doing is just a drop in the ocean. But the ocean would be less because of that missing drop.
- We think sometimes that poverty is only being hungry, naked and homeless. The poverty of being unwanted, unloved and uncared for is the greatest poverty. We must start in our own homes to remedy this kind of poverty.

Chapter 4:
Plans and Goals

Antoine de Saint-Exupéry (1900–1944) was a French writer and aviator. He disappeared on the night of July 31, 1944, while flying on a mission to collect data on German troop movements.

- A goal without a plan is just a wish.
- The meaning of things lies not in the things themselves but in our attitude toward them.

Peter Drucker (1909–2005) was a writer, management consultant, and university professor.

- Most of what we call management consists of making it difficult for people to get their work done.
- Plans are only good intentions unless they immediately degenerate into hard work.

Unknown TV announcer

- An idiot with a plan can beat a genius without a plan.

James Cash Penney (1875–1971) was an author, lecturer, and world traveler as well as the founder of the J. C. Penney Company in 1902.

- Long-range goals keep you from being frustrated by short-term failure

Henry Ford (1863–1947) was the American founder of the Ford Motor Company and the father of modern assembly lines used in mass production. His introduction of the Model T automobile revolutionized transportation and the American industry. He was a prolific inventor and was awarded 161 US patents. He became one of the richest and best known people in the world. Ford left most of his vast wealth to the Ford Foundation but arranged for his family to control the company permanently.

- Anyone who stops learning is old, whether at twenty or eighty. Anyone who keeps learning stays young. The greatest thing in life is to keep your mind young.
- As we advance in life, we learn the limits of our abilities.
- Any color—so long as it is black.
- Capital punishment is as fundamentally wrong as a cure for crime as charity is wrong as a cure for poverty.
- Enthusiasm is the yeast that makes your hopes shine to the stars. Enthusiasm is the sparkle in your eyes, the swing in your gait. The grip of your hand, the irresistible surge of will and energy to execute your ideas.
- Even a mistake may turn out to be the one thing necessary to a worthwhile achievement.
- Exercise is bunk. If you are healthy, you don't need it; if you are sick, you should not take it.
- Failure is simply the opportunity to begin again, this time more intelligently.
- I am looking for a lot of men who have an infinite capacity to not know what can't be done.

Earl Nightingale (1921–1989) was an American motivational speaker.

- People with goals succeed because they know where they're going.
- Whenever we're afraid, it's because we don't know enough. If we understood enough, we would never be afraid.
- Ideas are elusive, slippery things. Best to keep a pad of paper at your bedside, so you can stab them during the night before they get away. Everything begins with an idea.
- The mind moves in the direction of our currently dominant thoughts.
- All you need is the plan, the road map, and the courage to press on to your destination.
- You can feel successful and literally be successful regardless of whether or not you are making money.
- Don't let fear stand in the way of accomplishing anything.

Victor-Marie Hugo (1802–1885) was a French poet, playwright, novelist, essayist, artist, *statesman, human rights* activist, *and exponent of the Romantic movement in France. In France, Hugo's literary fame comes first from his poetry but also rests upon his novels and his dramatic achievements. Among many volumes of poetry,* Les Contemplations *and* La Légende des siècles *stand particularly high in critical esteem, and Hugo is sometimes identified as the greatest French poet. Outside France, his best-known works are the novels* Les Misérables *and* Notre-Dame de Paris *(known in English also as* The Hunchback of Notre-Dame*).*

- A man is not idle because he is absorbed in thought. There is a visible labor, and there is an invisible labor.
- Almost all our desires, when examined, contain something too shameful to reveal.
- Courage is the discovery that you may win, and trying when you know you can lose.
- The unreal is more powerful than the real, because nothing is as perfect as you can imagine it, because it's only intangible ideas, concepts, beliefs, fantasies that last. Stone crumbles, wood rots, people, well, they die. But things as fragile as a thought, a dream, a legend, they can go on and on.
- If death meant just leaving the stage long enough to change costumes and come back as a new character ... would you slow down? Or speed up?
- There are thoughts which are prayers. There are moments when, whatever the posture of the body, the soul is on its knees.
- People do not lack strength; they lack will.
- When a woman is talking to you, listen to what she says with her eyes.

Ralph Nader (1934–) is an attorney, a progressive political activist, and a five-time candidate for President of the United States.

- Three things tell a man: his eyes, his friends and his favorite quotes.
- Your best teacher is your last mistake.

- A leader has the vision and conviction that a dream can be achieved. He inspires the power and energy to get it done.
- The use of solar energy has not been opened up because the oil industry does not own the sun.
- Addiction should never be treated as a crime. It has to be treated as a health problem. We do not send alcoholics to jail in this country. Over 500,000 people are in our jails who are nonviolent drug users.

Chapter 5:
Love Galore

Erich Segal (1917–2010) was an American author, screenwriter, and educator.

- Love means never having to say you're sorry.

David Grayson (1964–) was an American football player.

- Looking back, I have this to regret, that too often when I loved, I did not say so.
- Goodness is uneventful. It does not flash, it glows.
- Talk of joy: there may be things better than beef stew and baked potatoes and home-made bread—there may be.
- A large volume of adventures may be grasped within this little span of life, by him who interests his heart in everything.

Victor-Marie Hugo (1802–1885) was a French poet, playwright, novelist, and essayist.

- The supreme happiness in life is the conviction that we are loved—loved for ourselves, or rather, loved in spite of ourselves.
- Love never dies a natural death. It dies because we don't know how to replenish its source. It dies of blindness and errors and betrayals. It dies of illness and wounds; it dies of weariness, of withering, of tarnishing.
- A mother's arms are made of tenderness, and children sleep soundly in them.
- The first symptom of love in a young man is shyness; the first symptom in a woman is boldness.
- Music expresses that which cannot be said and on which it is impossible to be silent.

Carl Jung (1875–1961), Swiss psychiatrist and influential thinker, was the founder of analytical psychology.

- Where love rules, there is no will to power, and where power predominates, love is lacking.

William Shakespeare *(1564–1616)*

- O Romeo, Romeo! Wherefore art thou Romeo?
  Deny thy father and refuse thy name;
  Or, if thou wilt not, be but sworn my love ...
  'Tis but thy name that is my enemy: ...
  What's in a name? That which we call a rose
  By any other word would smell as sweet ...
  (*Romeo and Juliet*, Act II, scene II)

William Congreve (1670–1729) was an English playwright and poet.

- Heaven has no rage like love to hatred returned,
  nor hell a fury like a woman scorned.

Karl Wallenda (1905–1978) was the founder of the Flying Wallendas, an internationally known daredevil circus act famous for performing death-defying stunts without a safety net. In 1947 they developed the unequaled three-tier, seven-man pyramid. In 1970, a sixty-five-year-old Karl performed a high-wire walk across the Tallulah Gorge formed by the Tallulah River in Georgia. An estimated thirty thousand people watched Karl perform two headstands as he crossed the quarter-mile-wide gap. In 1978, at age seventy-three, Karl attempted a walk between the two towers of the ten-story Condado Plaza Hotel in San Juan, Puerto Rico, on a wire stretched thirty-seven meters (121 feet) above the pavement, but fell to his death when winds exceeded forty-eight kilometers per hour. (Note: Two of his sons, Karl and Hugh, were my Kappa Sigma fraternity brothers at the University of Florida in 1946.)

- Being on the tightrope is living; everything else is waiting.

Chapter 6:
Dreams

Samuel Taylor Coleridge (1772–1834) was an English poet, critic, and philosopher who was, along with his friend William Wadsworth, one of the founders of the Romantic movement in England and one of the Lake Poets. He is probably best known for his poems "The Rime of the Ancient Mariner" and "Kubla Khan."

- What if you slept? And what if, in your sleep, you dreamed? And what if, in your dream, you went to heaven and there plucked a strange and beautiful flower? And what if, when you awoke, you had the flower in your hand? Ah, what then?

Yamamoto Tsunetomo (1659–1719) was a samurai. He is also known as Yamanoto Jocho, a name he took after retiring and becoming a monk.

- It is a good viewpoint to see the world as a dream. When you have something like a nightmare, you will wake up and tell yourself that it was only a dream. It is said that the world we live in is not a bit different from this.

James Allen (1864–1912) was a philosophical writer of British nationality, known for his inspirational books and poetry.

- The greatest achievements were at first and for a time dreams. The oak sleeps in an acorn.

George Washington Carver (1864–1943) was an American botanical researcher and agronomy educator who worked in agricultural extension at the Tuskegee Institute in Tuskegee, Alabama, teaching former slaves farming techniques for self-sufficiency.

- Most people search high and wide for the key to success. If they only knew, the key to their dreams lies within.

Martin Luther King Jr (1929–1968) was one of the main leaders of the American civil rights movement. His doctoral degree came from Boston University in 1955. He was the youngest man to ever receive the Nobel Peace Prize, in 1964 at age thirty-five. He is perhaps best noted for the "I have a dream" and "I've been to the mountaintop" speeches. He was assassinated April 4, 1968.

- I have a dream that one day this nation will rise up and live out the true meaning of its creed: "We hold these truths to be self-evident, that all men are created equal" ...
- Darkness cannot drive out darkness; only light can do that. Hate cannot drive out hate; only love can do that. Hate multiplies violence, and toughness multiplies toughness in a descending spiral of destruction ... The chain reaction of evil—hate begetting hate, wars producing more wars—must be broken, or we shall plunge into the dark abyss of annihilation.
- We must combine the toughness of the serpent and the softness of the dove, a tough mind and a tender heart.
- Man was born into barbarism when killing his fellow man was a normal condition of existence. And he has now reached the day when violence toward another human being must become as abhorrent as eating another's flesh.
- The curse of poverty has no justification in our age. It is socially as cruel and blind as the practice of cannibalism at the dawn of civilization when men ate each other because they had not yet learned to take food from the soil or to consume the abundant animal life around them. The time has come for us to civilize ourselves by the total, direct, and immediate abolition of poverty.

Archibald MacLeish (1892–1982) was an American poet, writer, and Librarian of Congress. He was awarded the Pulitzer Prize three times.

- There are those who will say that the liberation of humanity, the freedom of man and mind is nothing but a dream. They are right. It is the American dream.

Dan Rather (1931–) was anchor of the CBS Evening News *for twenty-four years.*

- Most people are looking for security, a nice, safe, prosperous future. And there is nothing wrong with that. It's called the American dream.
- The American dream is one of the greatest ideas in the history of human achievement ... It thrives today in an age when its core components of freedom and opportunity are open to more Americans than ever before. It holds a real, identifiable place in the American heart and mind, and it informs the aspirations of everyone from farmers to software developers, from detectives to bankers, from soldiers to social workers ... It defines us as a people, even as we add to its meaning with each new chapter in our national experience and our individual actions.

Chapter 7:
Aging—Like Good Beef, Fine Wine, and Old Folks

*Jack **Benny** (1894–1974) was an American comedian, vaudeville performer, and radio, television, and film actor. He was known for his ability to get laughs with either a pregnant pause or a single expression, such as his signature exasperated "Well."*

- Growing old is a case of mind over matter. If you don't mind, it doesn't matter.

*George **Burns** (1896–1996) was an Academy Award–winning Jewish-American comedian, actor, and writer.*

- You can't help getting older, but you don't have to get old.
- If you live to be one hundred, you've got it made. Very few people die past that age.
- I honestly think it is better to be a failure at something you love than to be a success at something you hate.

*Mickey **Mantle** (1931–1995) was inducted into the National Baseball Hall of Fame in 1974. He played his entire eighteen-year major-league professional career for the New York Yankees. He still holds the records for most World Series home runs (18), RBIs (40), runs (42), walks (43), extra-base hits (26), and total bases (123).*

- If I knew I was going to live this long, I'd have taken better care of myself.

*Bette **Davis** (1908–1989) was a two-time Academy Award–winning American actress of film, television, and theatre.*

- Old age ain't no place for sissies.

Investor's Business Daily

- Older people have had so many experiences that new occurrences rarely stimulate their minds.

Aristotle

- Old age, believe me, is a good and pleasant thing. It is true you are gently shouldered off the stage, but then you are given a comfortable front stall as a spectator.
- It is the mark of an educated mind to be able to entertain a thought without accepting it.

Holbrook Jackson (1874–1948) was a British journalist, writer, and publisher. He was recognized as one of the leading bibliophiles of his time.

- No man is ever old enough to know better.

Milton Berle (1908–2002) was an Emmy-winning American comedian and actor. He was the first major star of television and as such became known as Uncle Miltie or Mr. Television to millions during TV's golden age.

- I can't tell you his age, but when he was born the wonder drug was Mercurochrome.

Lucille Ball (1911–1989) was an iconic American comedienne; film, television, stage, and radio actress; glamour girl; and star of landmark sitcoms, such as I Love Lucy. *She was one of America's favorite stars and had one of Hollywood's longest careers. She received thirteen Emmy Award nominations and had four wins.*

- The secret of staying young is to live honestly, eat slowly, and lie about your age.

Jean Sibelius (1865-1957) was a Finnish composer of the later Romantic period and one of the most notable composers of the late nineteenth and early twentieth centuries.

- Every day in my old age is more important than I can say. It will never return. When one takes one's leave of life, one notices how much one has left undone.

Jeremy Schwartz (1971–), radiant Jeremy Schwartz, grew up in Plano, Texas.

- Live every day as if it were your last, because one of these, it will be.

REMEMBER:

> Old folks are worth a fortune
> With silver in their hair
> Gold in their teeth
> Stones in their kidneys
> Lead in their feet and
> Gas in their stomachs

VFW POST 8696 Palm Coast, Fl. Newsletter.

- A veteran is someone who, at one point in his life, wrote a blank check payable to "The United States of America" for an amount of "up to and including my life."

Chapter 8:
Business Sense

Andy Warhol (1928–1987) was the American artist most identified with pop art. The media called him the Prince of Pop.

- Being good in business is the most fundamental kind of art.

Unknown author

- A positive attitude is a magnet for positive results.

William Wrigley Jr (1861–1932), was a US chewing gum industrialist. He was founder of the Wm. Wrigley Jr Company.

- When two men in business always agree, one of them is unnecessary.

Alan Sugar (1947–), properly Sir Alan Michael Sugar, is a British businessman. He started selling car aerials and electrical goods out of a van he had bought with his savings of 100 pounds. He has now an estimated fortune of 830 million pounds. Sugar now stars in the BBC TV series The Apprentice. *The series is based upon the American television show of the same name, featuring entrepreneur Donald Trump, which had already proven popular in the United States.*

- It's having the right stuff, in the right place, at the right time—and neither too much nor too little of it.

Don Worden (?) is an elderly stock market guru who provides online charts on all stocks.

- On good days and bad days in the stock market, there is one thing I keep in mind. Following an unusually sustained advance, there is more downside risk than upside potential. This is a lesson we can learn with little damage, or we can learn it the hard way.

- In reality, oxymoronic behavior isn't exactly rare in the stock market.
- A dollar today is worth more than a dollar tomorrow.
- Looking at the NYSE composite through the 90s, it is interesting to note that 10 percent retrenchments were rare and 20 percent very rare. Thirty percent didn't occur from the start of my data until 2002.
- Sometimes, the thing to do is to sit back, chew on a straw, and let the stock market wear itself out, like a wild horse in a corral.

Andrew Carnegie (1835–1919), a self-made man born in Scotland, was considered to be the world's richest man in his time. He is known for having built one of the most powerful corporations in United States history and, late in life, giving away most of his riches to fund libraries, schools, and universities in America, Scotland, and other countries throughout the world. Steel is where he found his fortune. He has often been referred to as a true "rags to riches" man.

- There is no use whatever trying to help people who do not help themselves. You cannot push anyone up a ladder unless he is willing to climb himself.
- As I grow older, I pay less attention to what people say. I just watch what they do.

Chapter 9:
Saying It Statistically

Woody Allen (1935–) is a three-time Academy Award–winning American film director, writer, jazz musician, comedian, and playwright.

- Ninety percent of success is just showing up.

Street Gospel

- It is a mathematical fact that 50 percent of all doctors graduate in the bottom half of their class.
- Ninety-nine percent of lawyers give the rest a bad name.
- Eighty percent of all Americans have investments in mutual funds, retirement funds, 401(k)s, and the stock market.
- Eighty percent of all options expire worthless. Ninety percent of people who trade options lose.
- A journey of a thousand miles starts with the first step.
- God's last name is not "Dammit."
- True religion is the life we lead, not the creed we profess.
- There is no such thing as a free lunch. Anyone who tells you otherwise is trying to sell you something.
- Never trust a fart.
- Marriage is the leading cause of divorce.

Motley Fools' *newsletter dated 7/20/07*

- The majority of investors don't beat the market, and that includes the managers of most actively managed funds (though there are exceptions).
- The average 65-year-old will live another 20 years, which means half of us will live longer [than 85]. So unless you're a 90-year-old bullfighter who smokes, plan on having a multi-decade life expectancy—and for a timeline like that, go with stocks.

Andy Rooney (1919–) is an American radio and television writer. He became most famous as a humorist and commentator with his weekly broadcast A Few Minutes with Andy Rooney, *a part of the CBS news program* 60 Minutes *since 1979.*

- The 50–50–90 rule: Any time you have a 50–50 chance of getting something right, there is a 90 percent probability you'll get it wrong.
- Nothing in fine print is ever good news.

Chapter 10:
Wise Sayings

Sir Walter Scott (1771–1832) was First Baronet and a prolific Scottish historical novelist and poet popular throughout Europe during his time.

- O, what a tangled web we weave when first we practice to deceive.
- For success, attitude is equally as important as ability.
- He is the best sailor who can steer within fewest points of the wind, and exact a motive power out of the greatest obstacles.
- Discretion is the perfection of reason, and a guide to us in all the duties of life.
- A rusty nail placed near a faithful compass will sway it from the truth, and wreck the argosy.
- Love rules the court, the camp, the grove, and men below, and saints above: For love is heaven, and heaven is love.
- O! many a shaft, at random sent,
  Finds mark the archer little meant!
  And many a word, at random spoken,
  May soothe or wound a heart that's broken.
- Of all vices, drinking is the most incompatible with greatness.

Tom Hopkins (birthdate not available) is an authority on the subject of selling. He is known as the nation's number-one sales trainer.

- Being miserable is a habit. Being happy is a habit. The choice is yours.
- An expert is someone who knows a lot about the past.

Shirley Kruse(1921–), Women's Air Corp pilot during WW2, is a personal friend.

- Here's to you as good as you are,

And here's to me as bad as I am,
But as good as you are, and as bad as I am,
I'm as good as you are as bad as I am.

Street Gospel

- I know you believe that you understand what you think I said, but I'm not sure you realize that what you heard is not what I meant.
- Smith, where Jones had had "had had," had had "had"; "had had" had had the examiner's approval. (This is grammatically correct.)
- The trouble with some women is that they get all excited about nothing, and then they marry him.
- One of the hardest things in life is to learn which bridge to cross and which bridge to burn.

J. Paul Getty (1892–1976) was an American industrialist and founder of the Getty Oil Company.

- If you owe the bank $100, that's your problem. If you owe the bank $100 million, that's their problem.

Bob Dylan (1941–) is an American singer-songwriter, author, musician, poet, and, of late, disc jockey.

- A man is a success if he gets up in the morning and goes to bed at night and in between does what he wants to do.

Henry A. du Pont (1838–1926), known as "Colonel Henry," was an American soldier and politician from Winterthur, near Greenville, in New Castle County, Delaware. He was the grandson of the founder of E. I. Du Pont de Nemours and Company, a veteran of the Civil War, and served two terms as US Senator from Delaware.

- If it ain't broke, don't fix it.

Leon Kass (1939–) is an American physician, scientist, educator, and public intellectual. He is known as a proponent of liberal education via the "Great Books."

- Many people recognize that technology often comes with unintended and undesirable side effects.

Hugh White (1773–1840) was a prominent American politician and a Senator.

- The past cannot be changed. The future is yet in your hands.

Brant Allen (1940–) is a philosopher posing as a fantastic boat mechanic and a personal friend.

- Left alone, we sink to our lowest point.
- The best engineering is one moving part or less.
- Silence is my favorite noise.
- Fear is not knowing, and anger is not loving.
- The hardest thing I have learned in life is to "shut up."
- Keep working, stay busy or else you can't.
- Rocks fall at random except for divine intervention.
- We live on faith until we learn the truth, and the Bible says, "The truth will set you free."
- Faith is to believe what you cannot see. The reward of that faith is to see what you believed.
- A grunt is worth 10 percent toward the total effort.
- I would rather be smart than lucky. Smart works all the time. Luck works at random.
- Certain events chase certain personalities.
- Anxious events chase anxious personalities.
- To listen is to see—to see is to know—and knowing is the experience we seek.
- I am trying to get smarter about my stupidity.
- Reality is that which, when you stop believing in it, doesn't go away.
- We all do voodoo ... only some of us are aware of it'

- You can be a butthead in this society and survive—most of my friends have.

John Steinbeck (1902–1968) was one of the best known and most widely read American writers of the twentieth century.

- It is a common experience that a problem difficult at night is resolved in the morning after the committee of sleep has worked on it.

Albert Szent-Gyorgyi (1893–1986) was a Hungarian-born biochemist. His medical university was originally established in Transylvania.

- Discovery of a solution consists of looking at the same thing as everyone else and thinking what nobody has thought.
- Water is life's matter and matrix, mother and median. There is no life without water.
- Whatever man does, he must first do in his mind.
- Here we stand in the middle of this new world with our primitive brain, attuned to the simple cave life, with terrific forces at our disposal, which we are clever enough to release, but whose consequences we cannot comprehend.
- A vitamin is a substance that makes you ill if you don't eat it.

Albert Einstein (1879–1955) was a German-born American physicist who developed the special and general theories of relativity. He won the Nobel prize for physics in 1921.

- Example isn't another way to teach, it is the only way to teach.
- Keep things as simple as you can but not any simpler.
- Common sense is the collection of prejudices acquired by age 18.
- Many of the things you can count, don't count. Many of the things you can't count really count.

- Only two things are infinite: the universe and human stupidity—and I'm not sure about the former.
- The only reason for time is so that everything doesn't happen at once.
- The only sure way to avoid making mistakes is to have no new ideas.
- If A equals success, then the formula is $A=X+Y+Z$, where X is "work," Y is "play," and Z is "keep your mouth shut."
- All things on our planet are in constant motion.
- Nothing happens until something moves.

Norman Cousins *(1915–1990) was a prominent political journalist, author, professor, and world peace advocate.*

- Wisdom consists of the anticipation of consequences.
- You are younger today than you will ever be again. Make use of it for the sake of tomorrow.
- Death is not the greatest loss in life. The greatest loss is what dies inside us while we live.

Paul Harvey *(1918–2009) was an American radio broadcaster for the ABC Radio Networks. His listening audience was estimated at 22 million people a week. He explained his enthusiastic support of his sponsors this way: "I am fiercely loyal to those willing to put their money where my mouth is."*

- In times like these, it helps to recall that there have always been times like these.

Edgar Allan Poe *(1809–1849) is noted for being the first well-known American writer to try to make a living by writing alone. It was not an easy choice, considering that the channels for writing and publishing in early America were in their infancy. He was best known for poetry. His recognition increased rapidly after he published "The Raven." Poe was paid only $9 for its publication. He is reputed to have had some health problems, including alcoholism.*

- Man's real life is happy, chiefly because he is ever expecting that it soon will be so.

- If you wish to forget anything on the spot, make a note that this thing is to be remembered.
- It is by no means an irrational fancy that, in a future existence, we shall look upon what we think our present existence, as a dream.
- All that we see or seem is but a dream within a dream.
- I became insane, with long intervals of horrible sanity.
- I have great faith in fools; self-confidence my friends call it.

Kenny Rogers (1938–) is a prolific American country singer, photographer, producer, songwriter, actor, and businessman.

- Know when to hold 'em, know when to fold 'em, know when to walk away, know when to run.

Aristotle (384–322 BC), Greek philosopher, was a student of Plato and teacher of Alexander the Great. He made important contributions by systemizing deductive logic and wrote on physical subjects. His philosophy had a long-lasting influence on the development of all Western philosophical theories.

- All human actions have one or more of these seven causes: chance, nature, compulsion, habit, reason, passion, and desire.
- A friend is a second self.
- Education is the best provision for the journey to old age.
- It is unbecoming for young men to utter maxims.
- Man perfected by society is the best of all animals; he is the most terrible of all when he lives without law and without justice.
- Poverty is the parent of revolution and crime.
- Anyone can become angry—that is easy. But to be angry with the right person, to the right degree, at the right time, for the right purpose, and in the right way—this is not easy.
- A friend to all is a friend to none.

Sophocles (495–406 BC) was the second of three ancient Greek tragedians whose work has survived to the present day. He wrote 120 or more plays during his life, but only seven have survived in complete form.

- Chance never helps those who do not help themselves.

Richard Schickel (1933–) is an author, journalist, and filmmaker.

- The law of unintended consequences pushes us ceaselessly through the years, permitting no pause for perspective.

Horace Greeley (1811–1872) was an American editor of a leading newspaper, a founder of the Liberal Republican Party, reformer, and politician. His New York Tribune *was America's most influential newspaper from the 1840s to the 1870s, and Greeley was known as the greatest editor of his day.*

- Fame is a vapor, popularity an accident, riches take wings. Only one thing endures, and that is character.

George Halas (1895–1983) was nicknamed "Papa Bear" and "Mr. Everything." He was a player, coach, owner, inventor, jurist, producer, philanthropist, philatelist, and pioneer in professional football and the iconic longtime leader of the NFL Chicago Bears.

- Nothing is work unless you'd rather be doing something else.

Sydney J. Harris (1917–1986) was an American science cartoonist.

- People who think they're generous to a fault usually think that is their only fault.

Shakespeare

- There is nothing either good or bad, but thinking makes it so. (*Hamlet,* Act 2, scene 2)

Abbas ibn Al-ahnaf *(750- 809) was an Arab poet. His work consists solely of love poems.*

- Four things come not back—the spoken word, the spent arrow, time past, and the neglected opportunity.

James Gould Cozzens *(1903–1978) was a Pulitzer Prize–winning American novelist.*

- He was quoted in a featured article in *Time* as saying, "I can't read ten pages of Steinbeck without throwing up."
- A cynic is just a man who found out when he was about ten that there is no Santa Claus, and he's still upset.

Neil Peart *(1952–) is a Canadian musician and author.*

- If you choose not to decide—you still have made a choice.

William Ralph Inge *(1860–1954) was an English author, Anglican priest, and professor of divinity at Cambridge.*

- Anxiety is interest paid on trouble before it is due.

Street Gospel

- Don't let people drive you crazy when you know it is in walking distance.
- Advice is often needed, but seldom appreciated.

Laurence J. Peter *(1919–1990) was an educator and "hierarchiologist," best known by the general public for formulating the Peter Principle.*

- In a hierarchy every employee tends to rise to his level of incompetence. [This is known as the Peter Principle.]
- It is wise to remember that you are one of those who can be fooled some of the time.
- It is easier to make money than to save it. One is exertion; the other, self-denial.

- Don't believe in miracles—depend on them.
- Speak when you are angry, and you will make the best speech you'll ever regret.
- Competence, like truth, beauty, and contact lenses, is in the eye of the beholder.
- If a cluttered desk is the sign of a cluttered mind, what is the significance of a clean desk?
- Psychiatry enables us to correct our faults by confessing our parents' shortcomings.

Eleanor Roosevelt (1884–1962) was an American political leader who used her influence as an active First Lady to promote the New Deal policies of her husband, President Franklin D. Roosevelt, as well as taking a prominent role as an advocate for civil rights. She was one of the most admired persons of the twentieth century, according to Gallup's List of Widely Admired People.

- I think, at a child's birth, if a mother could ask a fairy godmother to endow it with the most useful gift, that useful gift would be curiosity.

René Descartes (1596–1650) was a highly influential French philosopher, mathematician, scientist, and writer.

- Divide each difficulty into as many parts as is feasible and necessary to resolve it.

Roadside church signs across America

- Words can't break bones, but they can break hearts.

Oprah Winfrey (1954–) is an American actress and television talk show host.

- What we're all striving for is authenticity, a spirit-to-spirit connection.
- Whatever you fear the most has no power—it is your fear that has the power.

- I trust that everything happens for a reason, even when we're not wise enough to see it.
- Real integrity is doing the right thing, knowing that nobody's going to know whether you did it or not.
- What I learned about being angry with people is that it generally hurts you more than it hurts them.
- It is possible to do whatever you choose, if you get to know who you are and are willing to work with a power greater than ourselves to do it.

Ginger Rogers (1911–1995), born Virginia Katherine McMath, was an Academy Award–winning American film and stage actress, dancer, and singer. In a film career spanning fifty years, she made seventy-three films and is now principally celebrated for her role as Fred Astaire's romantic interest and dancing partner in a series of ten Hollywood musical films that revolutionized the genre.

- I don't know why everyone makes such a fuss about Fred Astaire's dancing. I did all the same steps, only backwards. And in heels!

Lily Tomlin (1939–) is an Academy Award–nominated actress, comedienne, writer, and producer. Her body of work has garnered her several Tony Awards and Emmy Awards, as well as a Grammy Award.

- The trouble with the rat race is that even if you win, you're still a rat.

W. Clement Stone (1902–2002) was a prominent businessman, philanthropist, and self-help book author. Stone is remembered for contributing $2 million to President Richard Nixon's election campaigns in 1968 and 1972; these were cited in congressional debates after Watergate to institute campaign spending limits.

- There is little difference in people,
  but that little difference makes a big difference.
  The little difference is attitude;
  The big difference
  Is whether it is positive or negative.

Fred Schwed, Jr (?) wrote a book, Where Are the Customers' Yachts? or A Good Hard Look at Wall Street.

- The average Wall Streeter, faced with nothing profitable to do, does nothing for only a brief time. Then suddenly and hysterically, he does something which turns out to be extremely unprofitable. He is not a lazy man.

Plutarch *(AD 46–120) was a Greek historian, biographer, essayist, and Middle Platonist.*

- Do not speak of your happiness to one less fortunate than yourself.
- Know how to listen, and you will profit even from those who talk badly.
- Perseverance is more prevailing than violence; and many things, which cannot be overcome when they are together, yield themselves up when taken little by little.
- For to err in opinion, though it be not the part of wise men, is at least human.
- The very spring and root of honesty and virtue lie in good education.
- When the candles are out, all women are fair.

Oscar Wilde (1854–1900) was an Irish poet, novelist, dramatist, and critic.

- Consistency is the last refuge of the unimaginative.
- To the soul, there is hardly anything more healing than friendship.
- A little sincerity is a dangerous thing, and a great deal of it is absolutely fatal.
- Illusion is the first of all pleasures.
- One should always play fairly when one has the winning cards.
- Morality, like art, means drawing a line somewhere.
- I am not young enough to know everything.
- It is always a silly thing to give advice, but to give good advice is fatal.

- The good ended happily, and the bad ended unhappily. That is what fiction means.
- Some cause happiness wherever they go; others, whenever they go.
- Be yourself; everyone else is already taken.
- I am so clever that sometimes I don't understand a single word of what I am saying.
- I love talking about nothing. It is the only thing I know anything about.
- A true friend stabs you in the front.
- Fashion is a form of ugliness so intolerable that we have to alter it every six months.

Warren Buffett (1930–), entrepreneur, ranks second on the World's Billionaires 2007. The "Oracle of Omaha"—the world's greatest stock market investor—lives in a house he bought for $31,500, dines on burgers, and quotes Mae West.

- I don't look to jump over seven-foot bars; I look for one-foot bars that I can step over.
- I violated the Noah rule: Predicting rain doesn't count; building arks does.
- Be fearful when others are greedy and greedy when others are fearful.

Arthur M. Schlesinger Jr (1917–2007) was an American historian and Pulitzer Prize recipient. He wrote a detailed account of the Kennedy administration entitled A Thousand Days.

- Economists are about as useful as astrologers in predicting the future, and, like astrologers, they never let failure on one occasion diminish certitude on the next.

Nicholas Zaharis (1921–) is an unrecognized Greek philosopher and personal friend.

- Women will spend hours looking in the mirror, putting on cosmetics for their boyfriend. When you compliment them, it is better than buying those flowers.

- Education is expensive, but ignorance is more expensive.
- Be happy. If you can't, make someone else miserable.
- No one knows what the turtle thinks but the turtle.

Ralph Lavoie (1921–2009) was a staff sergeant and ball turret gunner with the 384th Bombardment Group, Mighty Eighth Air Force, during World War II. He was an American prisoner of war in Stalag 17B.

- We have freedom of speech. We have freedom of religion. We have freedom from want. We have freedom from fear. If you want to know what the word *freedom* means, ask a former prisoner of war.
- Half the world is composed of people who have something to say and can't, and the other half have nothing to say but keep on saying it.
- In three words I can sum up everything I have learned about life: it goes on.

Viktor Frankl (1905–1997) was an Austrian neurologist and psychiatrist as well as a Holocaust survivor. He was the founder of logotherapy and existential analysis, the "third Viennese school" of psychotherapy. He was one of the key figures in existential therapy.

- For the meaning of life differs from man to man, from day to day, and from hour to hour. What matters, therefore, is not the meaning of life in general but rather the specific meaning of a person's life at a given moment.

Mary Kay Ash (1918–2001) was a US businesswoman and the founder of Mary Kay Cosmetics, Inc. At the time of her death, Mary Kay Cosmetics had over 800,000 representatives in thirty-seven countries, with total annual sales of over $2 billion at retail.

- Those people blessed with the most talent don't necessarily outperform everyone else. It's the people with the follow-through who excel.

Robert K. Greenleaf (1904–1990) was the founder of the modern servant-leader movement. The servant-leader concept is servant first for everybody. It begins with the natural feeling that one wants to serve, to serve first. Greenleaf's theory is that the more able and the less able should serve each other. It is the opposite of the leader who bosses by power alone. In other words, a servant-leader is a servant who happens to be a leader. The concept was introduced by Greenleaf in 1970, and now thousands if not millions of people in business occupations have heard the term "servant-leadership." In its simplest form, the servant concept simply means that everybody should be nice to everybody.

- Many attempts to communicate are nullified by saying too much.
- The difference between a boss and a leader: a boss says "Go!"—a leader says, "Let's go!"

Regina Brett *(1956–) is a newspaper columnist and author of* 45 Lessons Life Taught Me.

It took me 40 years to find and hold onto happiness. I always felt that at the moment I was born, God must have blinked. He missed the occasion and never knew I had arrived. My parents had 11 children. While I love them and my five brothers and five sisters deeply, some days I felt lost in the litter. I ended up confused by the nuns at 6, a lost soul who drank too much at 16, an unwed mother at 21, a college graduate at 30, a single mother for 18 years, and finally, wife at 40, married to a man who treated me like a queen. Then I got cancer at 41. It took a year to fight it, then a year to recover from the fight.

When I turned 45, I lay in bed reflecting on all life had taught me. My soul sprang a leak and ideas flowed out. My pen simply caught them and set the words on paper. I typed them up and turned them into a newspaper column of the 45 lessons life taught me.

These lessons were published in her daily column with the Plain Dealer *newspaper in Cleveland, Ohio. Something amazing happened. People across the country began to forward the column. Ministers, nurses, and social workers requested reprints to run in newsletters, church bulletins, and small town newspapers. People of all religions and those of none at all could relate. While some of the lessons speak of God, people found in them universal truths. I've heard from agnostics and atheists who carry the list of lessons in their wallets and keep it tacked to their work cubicles and stuck under refrigerator magnets. The lessons are posted on blogs and websites by people all over the world. All 45 lessons follow:*

Lesson 1: "Life isn't fair, but it is still good." People shouldn't get cancer, especially children. But even cancer can bring about gifts.

Lesson 2: "When in doubt, just take the next right step." This is a drug of choice to fight depression.

Lesson 3: "Life is too short to waste time hating everyone."

Lesson 4: "Your job won't take care of you when you are sick." Your friends and parents will. Stay in touch.

Lesson 5: "Pay off your credit cards every month."

Lesson 6: "You don't have to win every argument. Agree to disagree."

Lesson 7: "Cry with someone. It's more healing than crying alone."

Lesson 8: "It's okay to get angry with God. He can take it."

Lesson 9: "Save for retirement starting with your first paycheck."

Lesson 10: "When it comes to chocolate, resistance is futile."

Lesson 11: "Make peace with your past so it won't screw up the present."

Lesson 12: " It's okay to let your children see you cry."

Lesson 13: "Don't compare your life to others. You have no idea what their journey is all about."

Lesson 14: "If your relationship has to be a secret, you shouldn't be in it."

Lesson 15: "Everything can change in the blink of an eye. But don't worry, God never blinks."

Lesson 16: "Life is too short for long pity parties. Get busy living, or get busy dying." Even if you feel awful, switch couches and enjoy a different view from the window. Radiation treatments can sap your strength, but it can't touch the power you have to change your thinking.

Lesson 17: "You can get through anything life hands you if you stay put in the day you are in and don't jump ahead." Cancer taught me to live only in the day I'm in, in the moment I'm in. Some moments, I simply ground myself by touching the desk, the table, the wall wherever I am and say, "You're right here. Stay put in this moment."

Lesson 18: "Take a deep breath. It calms the mind."

Lesson 19: "Get rid of anything that isn't useful, beautiful, or joyful."

Lesson 20: "Whatever doesn't kill you really does make you stronger."

Lesson 20: "It's never too late to have a happy childhood. But the second one is up to you and no one else."

Lesson 21: "When it comes to going after what you love in life, don't take no for an answer."

Lesson 22: "Overprepare and go with the flow." I use it every day. It works great at work, at home, and on family holidays.

Lesson 23: "Burn the candles, use the nice sheets, and wear the fancy lingerie. Don't save it for a special occasion. Today is special."

Lesson 24: "Be eccentric now. Don't wait for old age to wear purple."

Lesson 25: "The most important sex organ is the brain."

Lesson 26: "Frame every so-called disaster with these words: in five years, will it matter?"

Lesson 27: "Always choose life." Give yourself the best odds by doing all you need to do to stay alive. Going through chemo is like investing money in a retirement account. You feel the hit right now, but later in life you get to reap the benefits.

Lesson 28: "Forgive everyone everything."

Lesson 29: "What other people think of you is none of your business."

Lesson 30: "Time heals almost everything. Give time time."

Lesson 31: "However good or bad a situation is, it will change."

Lesson 32: "Don't take yourself so seriously. No one else does."

Lesson 33: "Believe in miracles."

Lesson 34: "God loves you because of who God is, not because of anything you did or didn't do." This is my "get out of jail" card. No more being stuck in the bondage of me. I don't have to dazzle God by being perfect. I'm supposed to be my messy self. What a relief.

Lesson 35: "Don't audit life. Show up and make the most of it now."

Lesson 36: "Growing old beats the alternative—dying young."

Lesson 37: "Your children get only one childhood. Make it memorable."

Lesson 38: "All that truly matters in the end is that you loved." This is the guiding compass point of every day.

Lesson 39: "Get outside every day. Miracles are waiting everywhere."

Lesson 40: "If we all threw our problems in a pile and saw everyone else's, we'd grab our own."

Lesson 41: "Envy is a waste of time. You already have all you need."

Lesson 42: "The best is yet to come." Just when you are ready to give up, hang in there. The best could be inches or hours or mere breaths away.

Lesson 43: "No matter how you feel, get up, dress up, and show up."

Lesson 44: "Yield."

Lesson 45: "Life isn't tied with a bow, but it is still a gift."

Caleb Colton (1780–1832) was an English cleric, writer, and collector, well known for his eccentricities.

- True friendship is like good health; the value of it is seldom known until it is lost.

Carl Friedrich Gauss (1777–1855) was a German mathematician and scientist who contributed significantly to many fields, including number theory, statistics, analysis, differential geometry, geodesy, electrostatics, astronomy, and optics. He is ranked as one of history's most influential mathematicians.

- It is not knowledge, but the act of learning, not possession but the act of getting there, which grants the greatest enjoyment.

Kappa Sigma Fraternity

- Advice is often needed but seldom appreciated.

Robert Schuller (1926–) is an American televangelist, pastor, and author known around the world through the weekly Hour of Power *television broadcast that he founded in 1970. He is also the founder of the Crystal Cathedral in Garden Grove, California, where the program originates. He retired in July 2010.*

- A great drive, a powerful determination, and a consuming desire will easily compensate for little or no talent.

David Ewing is a Palm Coast machinist and boat mechanic who can fix anything.

- Brute force and ignorance will overcome just about anything.
- Great minds think alike, but fools seldom differ.

Joyce Brothers (1925–) is an American psychologist and advice columnist.

- Trust your hunches. They're usually based on facts filed away just below the conscious level.

Hans Hoffman (1880–1966) was a painter and master of Abstract Expressionism.

- Every creative act requires simplication. Simplication results from a realization of what's essential.

George S. Patton Jr (1885–1945) was known as"Old Blood and Guts." He was one of the most colorful generals of World War II. Patton went to West Point where he was an undistinguished student but a remarkable athlete. He served on the staff of General John J. Pershing during the 1916 pursuit of Pancho Villa in Mexico, and during World War I, Patton served in Europe. During World War II he served in North Africa and Sicily before becoming the commander of the Third Army.

- A good solution applied with vigor now is better than a perfect solution applied ten minutes later.
- America loves a winner. America will not tolerate a loser … That's why America has never lost and never will lose a war.
- A pint of sweat will save a gallon of blood.
- If I do my full duty, the rest will take care of itself.
- May God have mercy upon my enemies, because I won't.
- Success is how you bounce off the bottom.
- No sane man is unafraid in battle, but discipline produces in him a form of vicarious courage.
- Never tell people how to do things. Tell them what to do, and they will surprise you with their ingenuity.
- Many soldiers are led to faulty ideas of war by knowing too much about too little.
- You are never beaten until you admit it.

MG Luis E. Gonzalez Vales, USA (Ret) *There follows a quotation from the November 2010 issue of* Officer Review, *a magazine published by MOWW (the Military Order of the World Wars).*

- To be born free is an accident, but to remain free and die free is a lifelong pursuit. Freedom should never be taken for granted; freedom must be constantly renewed and preserved. Let us not forget that the freedom we enjoy today was bought at the cost of the sacrifices of many, who stood up to repel aggression and to defend our liberties.

Dr. Seuss *(1904–1991), born Theodor Seuss Geisel, wrote and illustrated a multitude of beloved children's books.*

- Don't cry because it is over. Smile because it happened.
- Sometimes the questions are complicated, and the answers are simple.

- Fun is good.
- You are in pretty good shape for the shape you are in.

H. L. Mencken (1889–1956) was an American journalist, humorist, and social critic famous for his biting, sharp wit.

- For every difficult problem there's a solution that's simple, neat, and wrong.
- It is hard to believe that a man is telling the truth when you know that you would lie if you were in his place.
- The older I grow, the more I distrust the familiar doctrine that age brings wisdom.
- When women kiss it always reminds one of prizefighters shaking hands.
- Puritanism: The haunting fear that someone, somewhere, may be happy.

Margaret Mitchell (1900–1949) won the Pulitzer Prize in 1937 for her book, Gone with the Wind. *More than 30 million copies were sold, making it one of the most popular books of all time. Clark Gable and Vivien Leigh starred in a movie version.*

- Life's under no obligation to give us what we expect.

Charlotte Brontë (1816–1855) was an English author best known for her book, Jane Eyre.

- Prejudices, it is well known, are most difficult to eradicate from the heart whose soil has never been loosened or fertilized by education: they grow there firm as weeds among rocks.
- Life is so constructed that the event does not, cannot, will not match the expectation.

Kate Chopin (1851–1904) was primarily a short-story writer.

- There are some people who leave impressions not so lasting as the imprint of an oar upon the water.

Anne Frank (1929–1945) was one of the most renowned Jewish victims of the Holocaust. She died of typhus in a Nazi concentration camp at age fifteen. She had been given an autograph book when thirteen years old and used it as a diary. The Diary of Anne Frank *was saved and has been translated into several languages.*

- How true Daddy's words were when he said: "All children must look after their own upbringing. Parents can only give good advice or put them on the right paths, but the final forming of a person's character lies in their own hands."
- Everyone has inside of him a piece of good news. The good news is that you don't know how great you can be! How much you can love! What you can accomplish! And what your potential is!
- How wonderful it is that nobody need wait a single moment before starting to improve the world.
- And Then They Came for Me.

Chapter 11:
Wisecracks

Sigmund Freud (1856–1939) was an Austrian neurologist and psychiatrist who founded the psychoanalytic school of psychology. Freud is commonly referred to as "the father of psychoanalysis," and his work has been highly influential, popularizing such notions as the unconscious, the Oedipus complex, defense mechanisms, Freudian slips, and dream symbolism—while also making a long-lasting impact on fields as diverse as literature, film, Marxist and feminist theories, and psychology. An enormously controversial figure during his lifetime, he remains the subject of vigorous and even bitter debate, with the value of his legacy frequently disputed.

- The great question ... which I have not been able to answer ... is "What does a woman want?"

Amelia Earhart (1897–Missing 1937, declared deceased 1939) was a noted American aviation pioneer, author, and women's rights advocate. She was the first woman to fly solo across the Atlantic Ocean. Earhart disappeared over the central Pacific Ocean near Howland Island during an attempt to make a circumnavigation flight of the globe in 1937.

- I want to do it because I want to do it.

Popeye the sailor man is a fictional hero notable for appearing in comic strips and animated films. He first appeared in a comic strip Thimble Theater *in 1929.*

- I yam what I yam, and that's all what I yam.
- I fights to the finish 'cause I eats me spinach.

Bill Thompson, boating friend.

- He ain't got no couth.

Fred Thompson (1942–) is an American politician, actor, attorney, lobbyist, columnist, and radio host.

- After two years in Washington, I often long for the realism and sincerity of Hollywood.

Bill Crow (1923–) was the navigator on our B-17 crew and a prisoner of war.

- I may have a few faults, but being wrong is not one of them.

William Feather (1889–1981) founded a successful printing business but was best known as editor of the company's William Feather Magazine.

- Some people are making such thorough preparations for rainy days that they aren't enjoying today's sunshine.
- Early morning cheerfulness can be extremely obnoxious.
- A hotel isn't a home, but it's better than being a house-guest.
- Setting a good example for children takes all the fun out of middle age.
- The wisdom of the wise and the experience of the ages are preserved into perpetuity by a nation's proverbs, fables, folk sayings, and quotations.
- The petty economies of the rich are just as amusing as the silly extravagances of the poor.
- One of the indictments of civilizations is that happiness and intelligence are so rarely found in the same person
- Some people are making such thorough preparations for rainy days that they aren't enjoying today's sunshine.

Ah Those Birsith (The middle letters are scrambled, but it's readable)

Aoccdnig to recaersh at an English uinevrtisy, it deosn't mttaer in what order the ltteers in a wrod flal; the only iprmoatnt thing is that the frist and lsat ltteer are in the rghit pclae. The rset can be a toatl mses and you can sltil raed it wouthit a porbelm. This is bcuseae we do not raed ervey lteter by itlsef but the word as a wlohe and the biran fguiers it out aynawy. (Ralph E. Gies)

Zelda Willis, Palm Coast Internet employee.

+ A ship in the harbor is safe, but that's not what ships were built for.

John G. Diefenbaker (1895–1979) was the thirteenth Prime Minister of Canada (1957–1963).

+ Freedom is the right to be wrong: not the right to do wrong.

Robert Quillen (1887–1948) was a very quotable American humorist, journalist, and cartoonist.

+ Discussion is an exchange of knowledge; argument is an exchange of ignorance.

Dick Brigham, DuPont co-worker and personal friend. His wife Peggy is President Herbert Hoover's granddaughter. She was a fantastic dowser for water and almost anything else.

+ Halitosis is better than no breath at all.

Doctor's Gospel

+ If it tastes good, spit it out.

Vin Scully (1927–), member of the Baseball Hall of Fame, has been the Dodgers' play-by-play announcer for more than a half-century, in both Brooklyn and Los Angeles.

+ Losing feels worse than winning feels good.

Josh Billings (1818–1885) was the pen name of American humorist Henry Wheeler Shaw. He worked as a farmer, coal miner, explorer, and auctioneer before going into journalism, and was compared with Mark Twain, but his reputation has not endured so well over time. Another claim for his fame is the Josh Billings RunAground which is the oldest bike, canoe/kayak triathlon in the world. It happens in Great Barrington, Massachusetts.

- The trouble with people is not that they don't know, but that they know so much that ain't so.
- Adversity has the same effect on a man that severe training has on a pugilist—it reduces him to his fighting weight.
- One of the rarest things that a man ever does is to do the best he can.
- Silence is one of the hardest arguments to refute.
- It ain't no disgrace for a man to fall, but to lie there and grunt is.
- Life consists not in holding good cards, but in playing those you do hold well.
- Life consists not in holding good cards but in playing those you hold well.

Will Rogers (1879–1935) was a Cherokee-American cowboy, comedian, humorist, social commentator, vaudeville performer, and actor. By the mid-1930s, Rogers was adored by the American people and was the top-paid movie star in Hollywood at the time. On an around-the-world trip with aviator Wiley Post, Rogers died when their small airplane crashed near Barrow, Alaska Territory in 1935.

- I don't make jokes. I just watch the government and report the facts.
- Buy a stock. If it goes up, sell it. If it doesn't go up, don't buy it.
- I belong to no organized party. I am a Democrat.
- Things ain't what they used to be and probably never was.
- Good judgment comes from experience ... and a lot of that comes from bad judgment.
- If you get to thinkin' you're a person of some influence, try orderin' somebody else's dog around.

Charles Schulz (1922–2000) was a twentieth-century American cartoonist known worldwide for his Peanuts *comic strip.*

- Don't worry about the world coming to an end today. It's already tomorrow in Australia.
- Nobody remembers who came in second.

Mark Twain was the pen name of Samuel Langhorne Clemens (1835–1910). Mark Twain was an American humanist, humorist, satirist, lecturer, and writer. He is most noted for his novels Adventures of Huckleberry Finn, *which has since been called the Great American Novel, and* The Adventures of Tom Sawyer. *Twain enjoyed immense public popularity. American author William Faulkner called Twain "the father of American literature."*

- Noise proves nothing. Often a hen who has merely laid an egg cackles as if she had laid an asteroid.
- A man cannot be comfortable without his own approval.
- There is no sadder sight than a young pessimist, except an old optimist.
- At fifty, a man can be an ass without being an optimist but not an optimist without being an ass.
- Suppose you were an idiot. And suppose you were a member of Congress. But then, I repeat myself.
- Last week, I stated this woman was the ugliest woman I had ever seen. I have since been visited by her sister and now wish to withdraw that statement.
- There are two times in a man's life when he should not speculate: when he can't afford it and when he can.
- Opportunity does not just come along—it is there all the time—we just have to see it.
- Anger is an acid that can do more harm to the vessel in which it is stored than to anything on which it is poured.
- Apparently there is nothing that cannot happen today.

Joe Moore (1951–) has been an American educator, academic administrator, and news commentator.

- To most of us, the leading economic indicator is our bank account.

James Thurber (1894–1961) was an American author, cartoonist, humorist, and satirist.

- Well, if I called the wrong number, why did you answer the phone?

H. Stanley Judd (1950–) was a British Lord. The Stanley Cup (trophy), to be presented annually to the champion NHL hockey team, was named to honor him.

- It's a little like wrestling a gorilla. You don't quit when you are tired—you quit when the gorilla is tired.
- Without goals and plans to reach them, you are like a ship that has set sail with no destination.
- A good plan today is better than a perfect plan tomorrow.
- It's not the plan that is important, it's the planning. Graeme Edwards, Dwight Eisenhower, and George Patton stated similarly.

Spike Milligan (1918–2002) was a British comedian and humorous writer. He was considered an extraordinary twentieth-century comic genius.

- Money can't buy you happiness, but it does bring you a more pleasant form of misery.
- All I ask is a chance to prove that money can't make me happy.
- I'm not afraid of dying. I just don't want to be there when it happens.

Jimmy Buffett (1946–) is a singer, songwriter, author, businessman, and recently a film producer. He was initiated into the Kappa Sigma fraternity at the University of Southern Mississippi.

- Indecision may or may not be my problem.
- We are the people our parents warned us about.
- If the phone doesn't ring, it's me. (song title)

Mae West (1893–1980) was an American actress noted for her sly or broad on-screen humor.

- It's not the men in my life but the life in my men.
- I generally avoid temptation unless I can't resist it.
- His mother should have thrown him away and kept the stork.
- Too much of a good thing is wonderful.
- Between two evils, I always pick the one I never tried before.
- Marriage is a great institution, but I am not ready for an institution yet.
- I have found men who didn't know how to kiss.
- A man can be short and dumpy and getting bald, but if he has fire, women will like him.

George Bernard Shaw (1856–1950), world-famous playwright born in Dublin and a Nobel Prize Laureate in literature, was the son of a civil servant.

- England and America are two countries separated by a common language.
- A lifetime of happiness! No man alive could bear it; it would be hell on earth.
- Hegel was right when he said that we learn from history that man can never learn anything from history.
- If all economists were laid end to end, they would not reach a conclusion.
- Lack of money is the root of all evil.
- The liar's punishment is not in the least that he is not believed but that he cannot believe anyone else.
- If you have an apple and I have an apple, and we exchange these apples, then you and I will each have one apple. But if you have an idea and I have an idea, and we exchange these ideas, each of us will have two ideas.

Harry Orwig (1923–2003) was a high school classmate and everybody's best friend.

- AB? CD puppies? LMNO Puppies. OSAR! CMPN?

Antoine de Saint-Exupéry

- The meaning of things lies not in the things themselves but in our attitude toward them.

Sir Winston Churchill *(1874–1965) was a British politician and statesman known for his leadership of the United Kingdom during the Second World War. He was widely regarded as one of the great wartime leaders. He served as Prime Minister from 1940 to 1945 and again from 1951 to 1955.*

- You can always count on Americans to do the right thing—after they've tried everything else.
- A man does what he must in spite of personal consequences, in spite of obstacles and danger and pressures ... and that is the basis of all human morality. [In other words, "A man's gotta do what a man's gotta do."]

Charles Wadsworth *(1928–) is an international favorite, acclaimed both as a pianist and a music promoter.*

- By the time a man realizes that maybe his father was right, he usually has a son who thinks he's wrong.

John ?, *A Palm Coast house painter from Huntington, Long Island.*

- If you don't lie, you never have to remember what you said.

Katherine Whitehorn *(dates unknown)*

- The easiest way for your children to learn about money is for you not to have any.

Susan Marcotte

- Anger helps straighten out a problem as much as a fan helps straighten out a pile of papers.

Willie Sutton (1901–1980) had an amazingly successful career of fabulous bank robberies.

- The legendary Willie Sutton robbed banks because, as he famously explained, that's where the money was.

Charles Barkley (1963–) is a basketball legend and talk show host.

- Poor people have been voting for Democrats for the last fifty years ... and they are still poor.

Robert A. Heinlein (1907–1988) had a reputation as "the dean of science fiction." His writing career lasted almost fifty years, during which he wrote thirty-two novels and fifty-nine short stories.

- In the absence of clearly defined goals, we become strangely loyal to performing daily trivia until ultimately we become enslaved by it.
- Writing is not necessarily something to be ashamed of, but do it in private and wash your hands afterwards.
- The supreme irony of life is that hardly anyone gets out of it alive.
- Don't handicap your children by making their lives easy.
- Everything is theoretically impossible, until it is done.
- I am free because I know I alone am morally responsible for everything I do. I am free, no matter what rules surround me. If I find them tolerable, I tolerate them; if I find them too obnoxious, I break them. I am free because I know that I alone am morally responsible for everything that I do.
- You can have peace. Or you can have freedom. Don't ever count on having both at once.
- Never underestimate the power of stupidity.
- A human being should be able to change a diaper, plan an invasion, butcher a hog, conn a ship, design a building,

write a sonnet, balance accounts, build a wall, set a bone, comfort the dying, take orders, give orders, cooperate, act alone, solve equations, analyze a new problem, pitch manure, program a computer, cook a tasty meal, fight efficiently, die gallantly. Specialization is for insects.

Robert Frost (1874–1963) attended Harvard and Dartmouth but never graduated from a college. But he received forty honorary degrees including ones from Princeton, Oxford, and Cambridge. He also received four Pulitzer Prizes for poetry.

- Half the world is composed of people who have something to say and can't, and the other half have nothing to say but keep on saying it.
- In three words I can sum up everything I have learned about life: it goes on.
- A diplomat is a man who always remembers a woman's birthday but never remembers her age.
- A jury consists of twelve persons chosen to decide who has the better lawyer.
- Don't ever take a fence down until you know why it was put up.

New York City. A popular phrase in NYC in 1989 during an acute shortage of water (maybe also in other places and other times).

- If it's yellow, let it mellow;
  If it's brown, flush it down.

Yogi Berra (1925–) was a Hall of Fame catcher for the New York Yankees.

- If you don't know where you are going, you might wind up someplace else.
- Nobody goes there anymore. It's too crowded.
- When you come to a fork in the road, take it.
- It ain't over till it's over.
- Sometimes you can observe a lot just by watching

- Winning ain't everything, but it sure beats whatever is in second place.
- Its deejay' vu all over again.
- Baseball is 90 percent mental. The other half is physical.
- I didn't really say everything I said.
- What is it about baseball and illogic?
- If you can't imitate him, don't copy him.
- Half the lies they tell about me aren't true.
- Pair them in threes.
- There are some people who, if they don't already know, you can't tell them.

Samuel Goldwyn (1879–1974) came to the United States from Poland and became a famous Hollywood film producer. He originated these classic manglings of the English language, now called Goldwynisms.

- I'll give you a definite maybe.
- I never liked you and I always will.
- Include me out.
- For your own information, I would like to ask you a question.
- Anybody who goes to a psychiatrist ought to have his head examined.
- I may not always be right, but I am never wrong.
- It's more magnificent than mediocre.
- A bachelor's life is no place for a single man.
- In two words, im-possible.
- Go see it, and see for yourself why it shouldn't be seen.
- We have all passed a lot of water since then.
- When I want your opinion I will give it to you.
- Color television! Bah, I won't believe it until I see it in black and white.
- Give me a smart idiot over a stupid genius any day.
- Give me a couple of years, and I will make that actress an overnight success.
- I had a monumental idea this morning, but I didn't like it.

Chapter 12:
About Luck

Robertson Davies (1913–1995) was a Canadian novelist, playwright, critic, journalist, and professor. He was one of Canada's best-known and most popular authors and one of its most distinguished "men of letters."

- What we call luck is the inner man externalized. We make things happen to us.

Ecclesiastes 9:11 NIV

- The race is not to the swift or the battle to the strong, nor does food come to the wise or wealth to the brilliant or favor to the learned; but time and chance happen to them all.

Richard Wiseman (1952–2006) was Professor of Public Understanding of Psychology at the University of Hertfordshire in the United Kingdom. He started his professional life as a magician, before obtaining a PhD in psychology from the University of Edinburgh. He wrote several books and made a special study on luck. A recent poll revealed that he was the psychologist most frequently quoted in the British media. According to Richard Wiseman, these four principles can create good fortune in your life and career.

1. *Maximize Chance Opportunities:* Lucky people are skilled at creating, noticing, and acting on chance opportunities. They do this in various ways, which include building and maintaining a strong network, adopting a relaxed attitude to life, and being open to new experiences.
2. *Listen to Your Lucky Hunches:* Lucky people make effective decisions by listening to their intuition and gut feelings. They also take steps to actively boost their intuitive abilities—for example, by meditating and clearing their mind of thoughts.

3. *Expect Good Fortune:* Lucky people are certain that the future will be bright. Over time, that expectation becomes a self-fulfilling prophecy because it helps lucky people persist in the face of failure and positively shapes their interactions with other people.

4. *Turn Bad Luck Into Good:* Lucky people employ various psychological techniques to cope with and even thrive upon the ill fortune that comes their way. For example, they spontaneously imagine how things could have been worse, they don't dwell on the ill fortune, and they take control of the situation.

- Bad luck is funny—provided it's not happening to you.

Shirley Temple Black (1928–) is an Academy Award–winning actress most famous for being an iconic American child actor of the 1930s, although she is also notable for her diplomatic career as an adult. In later life, she became a US ambassador and diplomat.

- Good luck needs no explanation.

R. E. Shay

- Depend on the rabbit's foot if you will, but remember it didn't work for the rabbit.

Chapter 13:
Proverbs

Old Danish Proverb

- Bad is never good until worse happens.

Old Yiddish Proverbs

- If all men pulled in one direction, the world would topple over.
- God could not be everywhere, and therefore He made mothers.
- If rich people could hire other people to die for them, the poor could make a wonderful living.

Old Irish Saying

- Who gossips with you will gossip of you.

Italian Proverbs

- Speak of the devil and he appears.
- Anger can be an expensive luxury.
- Better give a penny than lend twenty.

Russian Proverb

- The wolf will hire himself very cheaply as a shepherd.

German Proverb

- Anger with power is folly.

Heraclitus (535–475 BC) was a pre-Socratic Ionian philosopher. He is known for his doctrine that change is central to the universe and that the Logos is the fundamental order of all.

- Nothing endures but change.

Albert Camus (1913–1960) was a French author and philosopher who won the Nobel Prize in 1957.

- Integrity has no need of rules.
- Don't walk behind me; I may not lead. Don't walk in front of me; I may not follow. Just walk beside me, and be my friend.

Plato (424–348 BC) was a classical Greek philosopher. Together with his teacher, Socrates, and his student, Aristotle, Plato helped lay the philosophical foundations of Western culture. Plato was as much influenced by Socrates' thinking as by what he saw as his teacher's unjust death.

- There are three classes of men; lovers of wisdom, lovers of honor, and lovers of gain.
- Mankind will never see an end of trouble until … powers of wisdom come to hold political power, or holders of power … become lovers of wisdom.
- The beginning is the most important part of the work.

Kahlil Gibran (1883–1931) was a Lebanese American artist, poet, and writer. He is the third best-selling poet in history after Shakespeare and Laozi (Lao Tzu).

- A little knowledge that acts is worth infinitely more than much knowledge that is idle.

Barry Farber (1930–) is a longtime radio talk show host.

- There is no reward in life without risk.

H. G. Wells (1866–1946) was an English writer most famous today for his science fiction novels. Wells and Jules Verne are each sometimes referred to as the father of science fiction.

- Adapt or perish, now as ever, is nature's inexorable imperative.

John Henry Newman (1801–1890) was an Anglican convert to Roman Catholicism who was later made a cardinal and in 1991 proclaimed "venerable."

- We can believe what we choose, but we are answerable for what we choose to believe.

J. K. Rowling (1965–) is renowned as the author of the Harry Potter books.

- It is important to remember that we all have magic inside us.

William Butler Yeats (1865–1939) was an Irish poet, playwright, and essayist.

- Education is not the filling of a pail, but the lighting of a fire.

Anonymous Proverbs

- Proverbs are short sentences drawn from long and wise experiences.
- Not all kinds of beauty inspire love; there is a kind which only pleases the sight but does not captivate the affections.
- Hunger is the best sauce in the world.
- Nature does nothing uselessly.

Chapter 14:
Poetically Speaking

Anonymous: *A passage from the Sanskrit:*

> If you think you are beaten, you are.
> If you think you dare not, you don't.
> If you'd like to win, but think you can't,
> It's almost a cinch you won't.
> Life's battles don't always go
> To the stronger or faster man;
> But soon or late the man who wins
> Is the one who thinks he can.

Kalidasa *(fifth century?) was a Hindu Indian considered to be the greatest Sanskrit dramatist and poet of his time. He is referred to as the Indian Shakespeare as Shakespeare is referred to as the English Kalidasa.*

> Look to this day, for it is life—the very life of life.
> In its brief course lie all the verities and realities of
> your existence: the bliss of growth, the glory of action,
> the splendor of beauty. Yesterday is already a dream, and
> tomorrow is only a vision; but today, well lived, makes
> every yesterday a dream of happiness and every tomorrow a
> vision of hope. Look well, therefore to this day.
> Such is the salutation of the dawn.

Fra Giovanni *(AD 1513)*

> There is nothing I can give you
> That you do not already have.
> But there is much that, while I cannot give it,
> You can take
> No heaven can come to us
> Unless our hearts find rest in today.
> Take heaven.

No peace lies in the future
Which is not hidden
In this present instant.
Take peace.
The gloom of the world is but a shadow.
Behind it, yet within our reach, is joy.
There is radiance and glory in the darkness
could we but see.
And to see we have only to look.
And so, at this time,
I greet you.
Not quite as the world sends greetings,
But with profound esteem.

Emma Lazarus (1849-1887), wrote a sonnet, "The New Colossus," in 1883. In 1903, it was engraved on a bronze plaque and mounted inside the Statue of Liberty.

Give me your tired, your poor,
Your huddled masses yearning to breathe free,
The wretched refuse of your teeming shore.
Send these, the homeless, tempest-tost to me,
I lift my lamp beside the golden door!

Charles Hanson Towne (1877–1949) was an active literary person. As a poet, he wrote "Around the Corner."

Around the corner I have a friend,
In this great city that has no end;
Yet the days go by and and weeks rush on,
And before I know it, a year is gone,
And I never see my old friend's face,
For life is a swift and terrible race.
He knows I like him just as well,
As in the days when I rang his bell,
And he rang mine. We were younger then,
And now we are busy, tired men:
Tired with playing a foolish game,
Tired with trying to make name.

100

"Tomorrow," I say, "I will call on Jim
Just to show that I'm thinking of him."
But tomorrow comes—and tomorrow goes,
And distance between us grows and grows.
Around the corner—yet miles away ...
"Here's a telegram sir, ..." *Jim died today.*"
And that's what we get, and deserve in the end:
Around the corner, a vanished friend.

Alfred, Lord Tennyson (1809–1892) was a Poet Laureate of the United Kingdom. He is best known for his poem "Crossing the Bar." Some say he was writing his own eulogy. Even today it is often quoted at funerals. It is quoted in its entirety below:

Sunset and evening star,
And one clear call for me!
And may there be no moaning of the bar,
When I put out to sea,

But such a tide as moving seems asleep,
Too full for sound and foam,
When that which drew from out the boundless deep
Turns again home.

Twilight and evening bell,
And after that the dark!
And may there be no sadness of farewell,
When I embark;

For tho' from out our bourne of Time and Place
The flood may bear me far,
I hope to see my Pilot face to face
When I have crost the bar.

- 'Tis better to have loved and lost than never to have loved at all.

Max Ehrmann (1872–1945) was an American attorney, writer and poet. He wrote the following poem which achieved fame only after his death.

DISIDERATA *(Latin: "things desired")*

Go placidly amid the noise and the haste,
and remember what peace there may be in silence.
As far as possible without surrender
be on good terms with all persons.
Speak your truth quietly and clearly;
and listen to others,
even to the dull and the ignorant;
they too have their story.

Avoid loud and aggressive persons;
they are vexatious to the spirit.
If you compare yourself with others,
you may become vain or bitter,
for always there will be greater and lesser persons than yourself.
Enjoy your achievements as well as your plans.

Keep interested in your own career, however humble;
it is a real possession in the changing fortunes of time.
Exercise caution in your business affairs;
for the world is full of trickery.
But let this not blind you to what virtue there is;
many persons strive for high ideals;
and everywhere life is full of heroism.

Be yourself.
Especially, do not feign affection.
Neither be cynical about love,
for in the face of all aridity and disenchantment,
it is as perennial as the grass.

Take kindly the counsel of the years,
gracefully surrendering the things of youth.
Nurture strength of spirit to shield you in sudden misfortune.

But do not distress yourself with wild imaginings.
Many fears are born of fatigue and loneliness.
Beyond a wholesome discipline,
be gentle with yourself.

You are a child of the universe,
no less than the trees and the stars;
you have a right to be here.
And whether or not it is clear to you,
no doubt the universe is unfolding as it should.

Therefore be at peace with God,
whatever you conceive Him to be,
and whatever your labors and aspirations,
in the noisy confusion of life keep peace with your soul.

With all its sham, drudgery, and broken dreams,
it is still a beautiful world.
Be cheerful.
Strive to be happy.

Saint Augustine (354–430) was a Latin-speaking philosopher and theologian. The city of St. Augustine, Florida, was named after him and claims to be the oldest city in the United States.

- Faith is to believe what you cannot see. The reward of that faith is to see what you believed.
- God loves each of us as if there was only one of us.
- Hear the other side.
- No eulogy is due to him who simply does his duty and nothing more.
- The purpose of all wars, is peace.
- There is no possible source of evil except good.

Chapter 15:
Musically Speaking

Jimmy Durante (1893–1980) was best known as the "Big-Nosed Comedian," He also was a hot piano player and bandleader. He became one of the most famous and lovable entertainers of the twentieth century. His famous sign-off was "Goodnight, Mrs. Calabash, wherever you are." Some of the song titles he helped make famous are listed below:

- Hello, Young Lovers
- I'll Be Seeing You
- I'll See You in My Dreams
- It Had to Be You
- The Glory of Love
- You Made Me Love You
- You're Nobody Till Somebody Loves You
- Bill Bailey (Won't You Please Come Home?)

Bing Crosby (1903–1977) was a popular singer and movie actor. He is credited with more than a half-billion records in circulation. Some of the song titles he helped make famous are listed below:

- Stardust
- Sioux City Sue
- Blue Eyes
- Don't Fence Me In
- When Irish Eyes Are Smiling
- You Are My Sunshine
- Silver Bells
- Let It Snow, Let It Snow, Let It Snow
- The Cool, Cool, Cool of the Evening
- White Christmas
- Empty Saddles
- Jingle Bells

Doris Day (1922–) was one of the popular postwar vocalists and a movie actress. Some of her songs are listed below:

- I'm Forever Blowing Bubbles
- Que Sera Sera
- It's Magic
- Sentimental Journey
- Till We Meet Again
- On the Street Where You Live

Glenn Miller (1904–1944) was a popular bandleader in the 1930s and 1940s who helped create the Big Band sound. He joined the army and led the Glenn Miller Army Air Corps Band. On a flight from England to France on a stormy night his plane disappeared over the English Channel. No trace was ever found. Some of the songs he was most noted for are listed below:

- Tuxedo Junction
- In the Mood
- Moonlight Serenade
- Chattanooga Choo Choo
- I've Got a Gal in Kalamazoo
- String of Pearls
- Pennsylvania 6-5000
- Elmer's Tune

Chapter 16:
Maxims (Ubiquitous and Original Sources are Unknown).

- This too shall pass.
- Booms tend to follow busts. Busts tend to follow busts.
- Things are much improved when forced to redo—on second effort.
- Unintended consequences usually follow all actions.
- Things need time to develop. It's better to let them happen than to force the occasion.
- History has a remarkable tendency to deliver prosperity after misery.
- Might is right, but will power dominates.
- Don't try to buy at the bottom and sell at the top. It can't be done except by liars.
- Most of the successful people are the ones who do more listening than talking.
- Age is only a number, a cipher for the records. A man can't retire his experience. He must use it. Experience achieves more with less energy.
- When one has a lot of qualities, he doesn't feel the need to brag.
- A man is known by the company he keeps.
- A friend in need is a friend indeed.
- A chain is only as strong as its weakest link.
- A fine appearance is a poor substitute for inward worth.
- You can't push a string.
- You can't force a golf ball no matter how hard you try.
- Sometimes the squeaky wheel gets oiled, sometimes it gets replaced.
- Politics is a spectator sport.
- Don't sweat the small stuff.
- Time is always present, but it waits for no one.
- Things tend to happen in threes. (No proof.)

Chapter 17:
Ten Commandments for Those Over 40

1. Focus on enjoying people, not on indulging in or accumulating material things.
2. Plan to spend whatever you have saved. You deserve to enjoy it and the few healthy years you have left. Travel if you can afford it. Don't leave anything for your children or loved ones to quarrel about. By leaving anything, you may even cause more trouble when you are gone.
3. Live in the here and now, not in the yesterdays and tomorrows. It is only today that you can handle. Yesterday is gone, and tomorrow may not even happen.
4. Enjoy your grandchildren (if you are blessed with any), but don't be their full-time babysitter. You have no moral obligation to take care of them. Don't have any guilt about refusing to babysit anyone's kids, including your own grandchildren. Your parental obligation is to your children. After you have raised them into respectable adults, your duties of child-raising and babysitting are finished. Let your children raise their own offspring.
5. Accept physical weakness, sickness, and other physical pains. It is part of the aging process. Enjoy whatever your health can allow.
6. Enjoy what you are and what you have right now. Stop working hard for what you do not have. If you do not have it, it's probably too late.
7. Just enjoy your life with your spouse, children, grandchildren, and friends. People who truly love you, love you for yourself, not for what you have. Anyone who loves you for what you have will just give you misery.
8. Forgive, and accept forgiveness. Forgive yourself and others. Enjoy peace of mind and peace of soul.
9. Befriend death. It's a natural part of the life cycle. Don't be afraid of it. Death is the beginning of a new and better

life. So prepare yourself not for death but for a new life with the Almighty.

10. Be at peace with your creator. For ... He is all you have after you leave this life ...

Chapter 18:
Dog Tales

Andy Rooney (1919–) is an American radio and television writer. He became most famous as a humorist and commentator with his weekly broadcast "A Few Minutes with Andy Rooney," a part of the CBS news program 60 Minutes *since 1979.*

- The average dog is a nicer person than the average person.

Dave Barry (1947–) is a bestselling American author who wrote a nationally syndicated column for the Miami Herald *from 1983 to 2005.*

- You can say any foolish thing to a dog, and the dog will give you that look that says, "Wow, you're right! I never would've thought of that."

Robert A. Heinlein (1907–1988) had a reputation as "the dean of science fiction." His writing career lasted almost fifty years, during which he wrote thirty-two novels and fifty-nine short stories.

- Women and cats will do as they please, and men and dogs should relax and get used to the idea.

Ann Landers (Esther "Eppie" Pauline Friedman Lederer) (1918–2002) wrote a popular syndicated advice column, Ann Landers, regularly featured in many newspapers across North America. People would write her letters to seek her advice concerning their personal problems, and she would publish her advice in her columns.

- Don't accept your dog's admiration as conclusive evidence that you are wonderful.

Herman Melville (1819–1891) was an American novelist, short story writer, essayist, and poet. His longest novel was Moby-Dick.

- No philosophers so thoroughly comprehend as dogs and horses.

Corey Ford (1902–1969) was an American humorist, author, outdoorsman, and screenwriter.

- Properly trained, a man can be dog's best friend.

Lewis Grizzard (1946–1994) was an American writer and humorist, best known for his humorous columns in the Atlanta Journal–Constitution.

- Life is like a dog sled team. If you ain't the lead dog, the scenery never changes.
- The most affectionate creature in the world is a wet dog.

Robert Benchley (1889–1945) was an American humorist noted for his understated comic essays, including From Bed to Worse.

- A dog teaches a boy fidelity, perseverance, and to turn around three times before lying down.

Ambrose Bierce (1842–1913) was an American editorialist, journalist, short story writer, and satirist, today best known for his short story "An Occurrence at Owl Creek Bridge" and his Devil's Dictionary.

- Reverence: the spiritual attitude of a man to a god and a dog to a man.

Gene Hill (1923–2005) was a regular columnist for Field & Stream.

- Whoever said you can't buy happiness forgot little puppies.
- We never really own a dog as much as he owns us.

Winston Churchill (1874–1965) was a British politician known chiefly for his leadership of Great Britain during World War II. He served as Prime Minister of the United Kingdom from 1940 to 1945 and again from 1951 to 1955.

- I like pigs. Dogs look up to us. Cats look down on us. Pigs treat us as equals.

Street Gospel

- Dogs have always been credited with the power of seeing supernatural influences, as well as ghosts, spirits, faeries, or deities, which are invisible to human eyes. Dogs are believed to be aware of the presence of ghosts, and their barking, whimpering, or howling is often the first warning of supernatural occurrences.
- If your dog doesn't like someone, you probably shouldn't either.
- My goal in life is to be as good a person as my dog already thinks I am.
- Let sleeping dogs lie.

Lord Byron (George Gordon Byron, 6th Baron Byron) (1788–1824) was an English poet and leading figure in Romanticism. He was regarded as one of the greatest poets and remains widely read. Lord Byron's fame rests not only on his writings but also on his life, which featured extravagant living, numerous love affairs, debts, separations, and allegations of incest and sodomy. He was famously described by Lady Caroline Lamb as "mad, bad, and dangerous to know."

- The poor dog, in life the firmest friend,
  The first to welcome, foremost to defend,
  Whose honest heart is still the master's own,
  Who labours, fights, lives, breathes for him alone,
  Unhonor'd falls, unnoticed all his worth,
  While man, vain insect hopes to be forgiven,
  And claims himself a sole exclusive heaven.
  —Inscription on the monument of
  his Newfoundland dog (1808)

Chapter 19:
When Insults Had Class

George Bernard Shaw to Winston Churchill

- I am enclosing two tickets to the first night of my new play; bring a friend ... if you have one.

Winston Churchill, in response

- Cannot possibly attend first night; will attend second ... if there is one.

John Bright *(1811–1889)*

- He is a self-made man and worships his creator.

Winston Churchill *(1874–1965)*

- A modest little person, with much to be modest about.

Moses Hadas *(1900–1966)*

- Thank you for sending me a copy of your book. I'll waste no time reading it.

Irving S. Cobb *(1876–1944)*

- I've just learned about his illness. Let's hope it is nothing trivial.

Rex Hudson, Money *magazine coach, in reference to a bad stock market on 9/21/01.*

- There is an old Chinese curse, or an insult: "May you live in interesting times." We may be getting there.

Chapter 20:
Prophetic Insights

Larry Swing (?) is the president of the popular day and swing trading site mrswing.com.

- Remember, if you keep doing what you've been doing, then you will probably keep getting what you've been getting.
- This too shall pass.

The History Channel

- All forms of life require energy.

Ben Franklin (1706–1790) was one of the most important and influential Founding Fathers of the United States of America. A noted polymath, Franklin was a leading author and printer, satirist, political theorist, politician, scientist, inventor, civic activist, statesman, and diplomat. He invented the lightning rod, bifocals, the Franklin stove, the carriage odometer, and a musical instrument. He invented the idea of an American nation, and as a diplomat during the American Revolution, he secured the French alliance that helped make independence possible.

- He who lives on hope will die a poor man
- Energy and persistence conquer all things.
- Anger is never without a reason, but seldom with a good reason.
- All mankind is divided into three classes: those that are immovable, those that are movable, and those that move.
- A penny saved is a penny earned.
- A place for everything and everything in its place.
- Any fool can criticize, condemn, and complain, and most fools do.
- A small leak can sink a great ship.

Henry Wadsworth Longfellow (1807–1882) specialized in lyric poems and became the most popular poet of his time. Some of his best were "Paul Revere's Ride," "Evangeline," and "The Story of Hiawatha."

- Age is opportunity no less than youth itself, though in another dress. And as the evening twilight fades away, the sky is filled by the stars invisible by the day.
- If we could read the secret history of our enemies, we should find in each man's life sorrow and suffering enough to disarm all hostility.

Ernest Hemingway (1899–1961) was an American author and journalist. He won the Nobel Prize in literature in1954.

- There are some things, which cannot be learned quickly, and time, which is all we have, must be paid heavily for their acquiring.

Danny Thomas (1912–1991) was an American nightclub comedian and television and film actor.

- Success has nothing to do with what you gain in life or accomplish for yourself. It's what you do for others.

Napoleon Hill (1883–1970) was an American author who was one of the earliest producers of the modern genre of personal success literature. He is widely considered to be one of the great writers on success.

- Patience, persistence, and perspiration make an unbeatable combination for success.
- What the mind of man can conceive and believe, it can achieve.

Stuart Wilde (1946–) has been referred to as both an urban mystic and a visionary. He has written seventeen books on self-help, self-empowerment, spirituality, and consciousness. He has also released many tapes and CDs for meditation and transcendence. His works have been translated into over 30 languages. Some think he is the greatest living metaphysic in the world today.

- Our life's journey of self-discovery is not a straight-line rise from one level to another. Instead, it is a series of steep climbs and flat plateaus, then further climbs. Even though we all approach the journey from different directions, certain aspects or characteristics are common to all of us.
- Simplicity is an enigma. Most people find it very complicated. It's a straight line from A to B. But it is abhorrent to the human mind. There ought to be a university course on simplicity. The problem is that the course would only last for fifteen to twenty minutes, and who would believe in a PhD who would do that?
- Heart trouble is a long-term emotional condition, caused by being too tight, lacking warmth, and not liking others. What's hereditary is not a faulty heart, but the lack of love.
- I found out bravery is not the absence of fear, it's being able to operate effectively when scared shitless.

Steven Covey *(1932–) wrote the best-selling book* The Seven Habits of Highly Effective People.

- While we are free to choose our actions, we are not free to choose the consequences of our actions.

Charles Handy *(1932–) is an Irish author/philosopher specializing in organizational behavior and management.*

- The moment will arrive when you are comfortable with who you are and what you are—bald or old or fat or poor, successful or struggling—when you don't feel the need to apologize for anything or to deny anything. To be comfortable in your own skin is the beginning of strength.

Sojourner Truth *(1797–1883) was the self-given name, from 1843,* *of Isabella Baumfree, an American abolitionist and women's rights activist. Truth was born into slavery in Swartekill, New York.*

- It is the mind that makes the body.

Hugh Walpole *(1884–1941) was an English novelist. He was knighted in 1937. Sir Hugh Walpole was a key member of an exclusive homosexual literary clique in 1930s London that also included Noel Coward and Ivor Novello.*

- Men are often capable of greater things than they perform. They are sent into the world with bills of credit and seldom draw to their full extent.

John Steinbeck *(1902–1968) one of the best known and most widely read American writers of the twentieth century.*

- It is the nature of man to rise to greatness if greatness is expected of him.
- It is a common experience that a problem difficult at night is resolved in the morning after the committee of sleep has worked on it.

Richard Koch *(1950–) is a former management consultant, entrepreneur, and writer of several books on how to apply the Pareto principle (80/20 rule) in all walks of life. Koch also used his concepts to make a fortune from several private equity investments made personally. In his second book on the phenomenon,* The Power Laws, *he discusses the 80/20 principle as a basic principle for how the universe works and sees the process of evolution, as described by Charles Darwin, as a special case of the 80/20 principle at work. He also emphasizes that the 80/20 principle should be combined with W. Brian Arthur's concepts of positive feedback and increasing returns. (Note: the 80/20 rule says that 80 percent of the distribution of sales will be done by 20 percent of the firms, for example.)*

- The few things that work fantastically well should be identified, cultivated, nurtured, and multiplied.

Martin Luther (1483–1546) was a German monk, theologian, and church reformer. His ideas helped inspire the Protestant Reformation and change the course of Western civilization.

- How soon *not now* becomes *never*.

Louis Aragon (1897–1982) was a French poet and novelist and a longtime political supporter of the Communist party.

- We know that the nature of genius is to provide idiots with ideas twenty years later.

Bill Bradley (1943–) is an American Hall-of-Fame basketball player, Rhodes Scholar, and former three-term Democratic US Senator from New Jersey.

- Becoming number one is easier than remaining number one.

Ed Bradley (1941–2006) was a TV news correspondent, most prominently as a longtime regular on 60 Minutes.

- No matter what you do, no matter what you achieve, no matter how much success you have, no matter how much money you have, relationships are important.

Friedrich Wilhelm Nietzsche (1844–1900) was a nineteenth-century German philosopher and classical philologist. He advanced the concept of the superman or overman (Übermensch) and wrote critical texts on religion, morality, contemporary culture, philosophy, and science. His key ideas include the death of God, perspectivism, the Übermensch, eternal recurrence, and the will to power. One of his philosophies was that "Might is right."

- Insanity in individuals is something rare—but in groups, parties, nations, and epochs, it is the rule.
- Man is the cruelest animal.
- No price is too high to pay for the privilege of owning yourself.

- To predict the behavior of ordinary people in advance, you only have to assume that they will always try to escape a disagreeable situation with the smallest possible expenditure of intelligence.
- The advantage of a bad memory is that one enjoys several times the same good things for the first time.
- Ah, women. They make the highs higher and the lows more frequent.
- All things are subject to interpretation; whichever interpretation prevails at a given time is a function of power and not truth.
- He who has a why to live can bear almost any how.
- Only sick music makes money today.
- In heaven all the interesting people are missing.
- It is hard enough to remember my opinions, without also remembering my reasons for them.

Ralph Waldo Emerson (1803–1882) was an American essayist, philosopher, poet, and leader of the Transcendentalist movement in the early nineteenth century.

- It is one of the most beautiful compensations of this life that no man can sincerely try to help another without helping himself ... Serve and thou shalt be served.
- Is it so bad, then, to be misunderstood? Pythagoras was misunderstood, and Socrates, and Jesus, and Luther, and Copernicus, and Galileo, and Newton, and every pure and wise spirit that ever took flesh. To be great is to be misunderstood.
- If a man write a better book, preach a better sermon, or make a better mousetrap than his neighbor, tho' he build his house in the woods, the world will make a beaten path to his door.
- The reward of a thing well done is to have done it.
- Let us treat men and women well; treat them as if they were real. Perhaps they are.
- The louder he talked of his honor, the faster we counted our spoons.
- That which we persist in doing becomes easier for us to

do; not that the nature of the thing itself has changed, but our power to do it has changed.

- Natural ability without education has more often raised a man to glory and virtue than education without natural ability.
- The only way to have a friend is to be one.
- For every minute you remain angry, you give up sixty seconds of peace of mind.
- Do not go where the path may lead; go instead where there is no path and leave a trail.
- It was a high counsel that I once heard given to a young person. "Always do what you are afraid to do."
- Finish each day and be done with it. You have done what you could; some blunders and absurdities have crept in; forget them as soon as you can. Tomorrow is a new day; you shall begin it serenely and with too high a spirit to be encumbered with your old nonsense.
- How do you measure success? To laugh often, and much; to win the respect of intelligent people and the affection of children; to earn the appreciation of honest critics and endure the betrayal of false friends; to appreciate beauty; to find the best in others; to leave the world a bit better, whether by a healthy child, a redeemed social condition, or a job well done; to know even one other life has breathed because you lived. This is to have succeeded.
- Don't be too timid and squeamish about your actions. All life is an experiment.
- For every gain there is a loss, and for every loss there is a gain.

Edward Hallowell (1935–2009) was a psychiatrist specializing in ADD. He explains ADD as a racecar brain with a braking problem. He was a frequent guest on shows like Oprah, The Dr. Phil Show, Today, 20/20, *and many more. He was the author of eighteen books including* Driven to Distraction, Crazy Busy, *and* Super Parenting for ADD. *He was a retired colonel with the US Army.*

- In order to do what really matters to you, you have to first of all know what really matters to you.

Napoleon Bonaparte (1769–1821) was a French military and political leader who had significant impact on modern European history. His campaigns are studied at military Napoleon academies all over the world, and he is widely regarded as one of history's greatest commanders. He became Emperor of France. His invasion of Russia in 1812 marked a turning point in his fortunes. The Sixth Coalition defeated his forces at Leipzig and then invaded France. The coalition forced Napoleon to abdicate in 1814, exiling him to the island of Elba. He returned to France less than a year later and regained control of the government prior to his final defeat at Waterloo in 1815. Napoleon spent the remaining six years of his life under British supervision on the island of St. Helena in the Atlantic Ocean.

• Never interrupt your enemy when he is making a mistake.

Nostradamus (1503–1566) was a French apothecary and reputed seer who published collections of prophecies that have since become famous worldwide. Nostradamus was not only a diviner but also a professional healer. Most of his quatrains deal with disasters, such as plagues, earthquakes, wars, floods, invasions, murders, droughts, and battles—all undated. Nostradamus enthusiasts have credited him with predicting numerous events in world history, such as the Great Fire of London, the rise to power of Adolf Hitler, and the terrorist attacks on the World Trade Center—but only in hindsight. There is no evidence in the academic literature to suggest that any Nostradamus quatrain has ever been interpreted as predicting a specific event before it occurred, other than in vague, general terms that could apply to any number of other events. Most academic sources maintain that the associations made between world events and Nostradamus's quatrains are largely the result of misinterpretations or mistranslations (sometimes deliberate) or else are so tenuous as to render them useless as evidence of any genuine predictive power.

Mayan Prediction: It has been predicted that a life-changing major event will happen December 21, 2012. Thoughts on the type of event range from "the sky will fall and end life on Earth" to just a major change of some sort, maybe something good and not a calamity. The

December 2012 date is when the Mayan calendar ends. That's all we know for sure.

Edgar Cayce (1887–1945) was an average individual in most respects: a loving husband, a father of two children, a skilled photographer, a devoted husband, Sunday teacher, and eager gardener. Every year thousands of people from all over the world become interested in the life work of this ordinary man. Countless individuals have been touched by the lifework of this man who was raised a simple farm boy and yet became one of the most versatile and credible psychics the world has ever known.

Cayce was an American who claimed to be a psychic with the ability to answer questions on a variety of past and future subjects while in a self-induced trance. Several times almost every day, for more than forty years, he would induce an out-of-body state of consciousness and reveal profound information on subjects including health, dreams, meditation, Atlantis, religions, and reincarnation, to name a few. He considered the most important part of his work to be personal contacts involving healing and theology.

But it was the information that Cayce revealed about the future for which he is probably best known. He provided information about the history of humanity from the very beginning to a time in the future when humans will evolve into beings with supernatural powers. He described a new era of enlightenment and peace when divinity within humans would be manifested on Earth. But before this "Kingdom of God" would rule the world, Cayce foresaw world events that can only be described as apocalyptic, a period of purification involving natural disasters that will dramatically alter the surface of the Earth—wars, economic collapse, and sociopolitical unrest. These visions of the future agree with what is known about prophecies from NDEs (near-death experiences).

Cayce maintained that Atlantis was an ancient civilization that was technologically superior to even our own and that its last surviving islands disappeared somewhere in the Atlantic Ocean some 10,000 years ago. He revealed that the size of Atlantis was equal to that of Europe. He also revealed that a vast number of souls who lived past *lives in Atlantis have been incarnating to America for a long time now to usher in a new area of enlightened human consciousness. (Some people say that if the lines in the palm of your hand form an A, you once lived in Atlantis).*

Sixty years ago, who could have known that terms like "meditation," "akashic records," "spiritual growth," "auras," "soul mates," and "holistic medicine" would become household words to hundreds of thousands?

Cayce became a celebrity toward the end of his life. Today there are thousands of Cayce students, and more than three hundred books have been written about Edgar Cayce.

- Analyze thy life's experiences, see thy shortcomings, see thy virtues. Minimize those faults, magnify and glorify thy virtues.
- From what may anyone be saved? Only from themselves! That is their individual hell. They dig it with their own desires.
- An error we refuse to correct has many lives. It takes courage to face one's own shortcomings and wisdom to do something about them.
- You'll not be in heaven if you are not leaning on the arm of someone you have helped.
- Each soul enters with a mission. We all have a mission to perform.
- For the earth is only an atom in the universe of worlds.
- The conquering of self is truly greater than if one were to conquer many worlds.
- Life is continuous, and is infinite.
- Death is not the grave as many people think. It is another phenomenized form of life.
- Synchronicity has to do with all things being interconnected in the universe, patterns of "the flow," getting indirect messages from God in odd ways. Everyone has experienced it, but some don't know it. Many people call it "coincidence." Some examples are like talking or thinking about something, then a song comes on the radio that relates to it, or a TV ad, news story or a friend calls

or drops by and starts saying something directly related to it. Often it's like God or Angels trying to get a message to us in their own way. Some people claim they have been visited by ghosts and had visual contact and direct conversations about matters of some importance. Once, I was driving our car on a lonely stretch of road in the wee hours of the morning. My wife and two sons under five years of age were sound asleep. I fell asleep. Then I heard my grandfather, who had been dead almost three years, shouting my name. I woke up in time to follow a curve in the divided highway. Otherwise, straight ahead was a twenty-foot decline into a patch of tall trees.

George Will (1941–) is a Pulitzer Prize–winning, conservative American newspaper columnist, journalist, commentator, and author.

- The nicest part about being a pessimist is that you are constantly being either proven right or pleasantly surprised.

Tom Macke (1932–) is one of my former golfing buddies who felt compelled to visit Las Vegas at least once a month.

- I'm getting better at playing blackjack in Las Vegas. I'm not losing as much as I used to.

Ann Richards (1933–2006) was an American politician and teacher from Texas and served as governor of Texas (1991–1995).

- One of the most valuable lessons I learned ... is that we all have to learn from our mistakes, and we learn from those mistakes a lot more than we learn from the things we succeeded in doing.
- Our understanding is not intellectual, but instinctive.

Oscar Wilde (1854–1900) was an Irish poet, novelist, dramatist, and critic.

- We are all a little weird, and life's a little weird, and when we find someone whose weirdness is compatible with ours, we join up with them and feel in mutual weirdness and call it love.

- Fashion is a form of ugliness so intolerable that we have to alter it every six months.

Robert Collier (1885–1950) wrote self-help and metaphysical books in the twentieth century.

- It is only through your conscious mind that you can reach the subconscious. Your subconscious mind is the porter at the door, the watchman at the gate. It is to the conscious mind that the subconscious looks for all its impressions.

Stephen King (1947–) is an American author of more than two hundred stories including over fifty best-selling horror and fantasy novels.

- Talent is cheaper than table salt. What separates the talented individual from the successful one is a lot of hard work.

Will Durant (1885–1981) was an American philosopher, historian, and writer. He is best known for writing, with his wife, Ariel Durant, The Story of Civilization.

- To speak ill of others is a dishonest way of praising ourselves.

Charles (Chuck) Swindoll (1934–) is an evangelical Christian pastor, author, educator, and radio and television preacher.

- Attitude is more important than the past, than education, than money, than circumstances, than what people do or say. It is more important than appearance, giftedness, or skill.

Shakti Gawain (1948–) is an author and proponent of what she calls "personal development." Her books have sold over 10 million copies, according to her website. Gawain is a passionate environmentalist.

- Problems are messages.
- I am convinced that life in a physical body is meant to be an ecstatic experience.
- Our bodies communicate to us clearly and specifically, if we are willing to listen to them.
- The universe will reward you for taking chances on its behalf.
- We will discover the nature of our particular genius when we stop trying to conform to our own or other people's models, learn to be ourselves, and allow our natural channel to open. What I am actually saying is that we need to be willing to let our intuition guide us and then be willing to follow that guidance directly and fearlessly.

Nelson Mandela *(1918–) is a former president of South Africa. Before his presidency, Mandela was an anti-apartheid activist and spent twenty-seven years in prison. Among opponents of apartheid in South Africa and internationally he became a symbol of freedom and equality. Since the end of apartheid, he has been widely praised, even by former opponents.*

- One of the most difficult things is not to change society— but to change yourself.

William Shakespeare

- All the world's a stage, and all the men and women merely players. They have their exits and their entrances, and one man in his time plays many parts, his acts being seven ages. (*As You Like It,* Act 2, scene 7)

George S. Santayana *(1863–1952), a lifelong Spanish citizen, was raised and educated in the United States. He was a philosopher who wrote in English and is generally considered an American "man of letters."*

- Advertising is the modern substitute for argument.

- There is no cure for birth and death, so enjoy the interval.

Confucius (551–479 BC), one of the most famous people in ancient China, was a wise teacher, philosopher, thinker, educator, and founder of the school of philosophy known as Ju or Confucianism, which is still very influential in China.

- Everything has its beauty, but not everyone sees it.
- Look at the means which a man employs, consider his motives, and observe his pleasures. A man simply cannot conceal himself.
- All human actions have one or more of these seven causes: chance, nature, compulsion, habit, reason, passion, and desire.
- To know what is right and not to do it is the worst form of cowardice.
- Choose a job that you love, and you will never work a day in your life.
- Life is really simple, but we insist on making it complicated.
- And remember, no matter where you go, there you are.
- It is easy to hate, and it is difficult to love. This is how the whole scheme of things works: all good things are difficult to achieve, and bad things are very easy to get.
- By three methods we may learn wisdom: first, by reflection, which is noblest; second, by imitation, which is easiest; and third, by experience, which is the bitterest.
- It does not matter how slowly you go, so long as you do not stop.
- No matter how busy you may think you are, you must find time for reading or surrender yourself to self-chosen ignorance.

Kevlin Dalton (born ca. 1988) was a friend of Daniel Dyer, a victim in a double murder. The story was reported by the Daytona Beach News–Journal *during July or August 2010.*

- I want something to happen. Everybody wants immediate

gratification. But this is a process; a long process. But what happens in the dark comes out in the light, and he'll get what he deserves. Whatever they give him on earth is nothing compared to what God's going to give him.

Charles Alexander Eastman (1858–1939) was a native-born American Sioux Indian who grew up to be a physician, a writer, and a national lecturer. He was actually born in a buffalo hide tipi near Redwood Falls, Minnesota. His father's name was "Many Lightnings."

- Friendship is held to be the severest test of character. It is easy, we think, to be loyal to a family and clan, whose blood is in your own veins.

US Armed Forces Well-Known Slogan

- The difficult we do immediately: the impossible takes a little longer.

P. J. O'Rourke (1947–) is an American political satirist, journalist, writer, etc. One source claims he is the most quoted living man in modern humorous quotations. He was an early proponent of Gonzo journalism (whatever that is). One of his best regarded pieces was "How to Drive Fast on Drugs While Getting Your Wing-Wang Squeezed and Not Spill Your Drink."

- If you think health care is expensive now, wait until you see what it costs when it is "free!"
- America wasn't founded so that we could all be better. America was founded so we could all be anything we damned well pleased.
- Because of their size, parents may be difficult to discipline properly.

Gary Brumback (1935–) These particular sayings are from my neighbor and personal friend. He is the author of the new and widely acclaimed book, *The Devil's Marriage: Break Up the Corpocracy or Leave Democracy in the Lurch* (Brumback 2011: Published by AuthorHouse).

- Our government doesn't track corporate crime or corporate welfare. Our government lets the former happen & spends our dollars for the latter.
- The Loophole Bar: where Houdini corporate lawyers gather to hatch escape hatches for their corporations' crime.
- Health insurance industry: America's corpocracy all profits ensured. If America were a true democracy: all citizens insured.

Chapter 21:
Wise Sayings by Our Founding Fathers

John Hancock (1737–1793) was a merchant, statesman, and prominent patriot of the American Revolution. He served as president of the Second Continental Congress and was the first and third governor of the Commonwealth of Massachusetts. He is remembered for his large and stylish signature on the United States Declaration of Independence, so much so that the term John Hancock *became, in the United States, a synonym for signature. Example: "Put your John Hancock on this line" (still used sometimes).*

- There, I guess King George will be able to read that. (Remark on signing the American Declaration of Independence.)
- The greatest ability in business is to get along with others and to influence their actions.

John Adams (1735–1826) was an American statesman, diplomat, and political theorist. A leading champion of independence in 1776, he was the second president of the United States (1797–1801). He was one of the most influential Founding Fathers of the United States.

- A desire to be observed, considered, esteemed, praised, beloved, and admired by his fellows is one of the earliest as well as the keenest dispositions discovered in the heart of man.
- In politics the middle way is none at all.
- I must study politics and war that my sons may have liberty to study mathematics and philosophy.

Samuel Adams (1722–1803) was an American statesman, political philosopher, and one of the Founding Fathers of the United States. Adams was a leader of the movement that became the American Revolution. He was a second cousin to President John Adams.

- The liberties of our country, the freedom of our civil

constitution, are worth defending against all hazards: And it is our duty to defend them against all attacks.

Patrick Henry (1736–1799) is known and remembered for his "give me liberty or give me death" speech and as one of the Founding Fathers of the United States. Along with Samuel Adams and Thomas Paine, he is remembered as one of the most influential, radical advocates of the American Revolution and republicanism.

• I know not what course others may take, but as for me, give me liberty or give me death!
• I like dreams of the future better than the history of the past.

Thomas "Tom" Paine (1737–1809) was an author, pamphleteer, radical, inventor, intellectual, revolutionary, and one of the Founding Fathers of the United States. He has been called "a corset maker by trade, a journalist by profession, and a propagandist by inclination."

• Those who want to reap the benefits of this great nation must bear the fatigue of supporting it.

Edmund Burke (1727–1797) was an Irish statesman, author, orator, political theorist, and philosopher. He is mainly remembered for his support of the American colonies in the dispute with King George III and Great Britain that led to the American Revolution.

• The only thing necessary for the triumph of evil is for good men to do nothing.

Chapter 22:
Wise Sayings by USA Presidents

George Washington (1732–1799) was the first US president.

- 'Tis better to be alone than in bad company.

Thomas Jefferson (1743–1826) was the third president of the United States (1801–1809). A polymath, Jefferson achieved distinction as, among other things, a horticulturist, statesman, architect, archaeologist, author, inventor, and founder of the University of Virginia. When President John F. Kennedy welcomed forty-nine Nobel Prize winners to the White House in 1962, he said, "I think this is the most extraordinary collection of talent and of human knowledge that has ever been gathered at the White House—with the possible exception of when Thomas Jefferson dined alone."

- Whenever you do a thing, act as if the whole world were watching.
- I am a great believer in luck, and I find that the harder I work, the more I have of it.
- In matters of style, swim with the current; in matters of principle, stand like a rock.
- Delay is preferable to error.
- The most valuable of all talents is that of never using two words when one will do.
- It is wonderful how much may be done if we are always working.

Abraham Lincoln (1809–1865) was the sixteenth president (1861–1865). Scholars now rank Lincoln among the top three American presidents. His assassination in 1865 was the first of a US president and made him a martyr for the ideal of national unity.

- If there is anything that a man can do well, I say let him do it. Give him a chance.
- You can fool some of the people all the time, and all the

people some of the time, but you cannot fool all of the people all the time.

- Nearly all men can stand adversity, but if you want to test a man's character, give him power.
- He can compress the most words into the smallest idea of any man I know.
- Better to remain silent and be thought a fool than to speak out and remove all doubt.
- It has been my experience that folks who have no vices have very few virtues.
- Whatever you are, be a good one.

The Gettysburg Address

Four score and seven years ago our fathers brought forth on this continent, a new nation, conceived in Liberty, and dedicated to the proposition that all men are created equal.

Now we are engaged in a great civil war, testing whether that nation, or any nation so conceived and so dedicated, can long endure. We are met on a great battlefield of that war. We have come to dedicate a portion of that field, as a final resting place for those who here gave their lives that that nation might live. It is altogether fitting and proper that we should do this.

But, in a larger sense, we cannot dedicate—we cannot consecrate—we cannot hallow—this ground. The brave men, living and dead, who struggled here, have consecrated it, far above our poor power to add or detract. The world will little note, nor long remember what we say here, but it can never forget what they did here. It is for us the living, rather, to be dedicated here to the unfinished work which they who fought here have thus far so nobly advanced.

It is rather for us to be here dedicated to the great task remaining before us—that from these honored dead we take increased devotion to that cause for which they gave the last full measure of devotion—that we here highly resolve that these dead shall not have died in vain—that this nation, under God, shall have a new birth of freedom—and that government of the people, by the people, for the people, shall not perish from the earth.

Theodore Roosevelt (1858–1919) was the 26th president (1901–1909). He was a historian, biographer, statesman, hunter, naturalist, and orator. His prodigious literary output includes twenty-six books, over a thousand magazine articles, and thousands of speeches and letters. He died in his sleep in 1919, at the age of sixty.

- Do what you can, with what you have, where you are.
- Whenever you do a thing, act as if all the world were watching.

Woodrow Wilson (1856–1924) was the 28th president, in office during World War I.

- I would rather lose in a cause that will someday win than win in a cause that will someday lose.

Calvin Coolidge (1872–1933) was the 30th president (1923–1929).

- Nothing in the world can take the place of persistence. Talent will not; nothing is more common than unsuccessful men with talent. Genius will not; unrewarded genus is almost a proverb.
  Education will not; the world is full of educated derelicts. Persistence and determination alone are omnipotent.
- The right thing to do never requires any subterfuge; it is always simple and direct.
- No person has ever been rewarded for what he received. Honor has been the reward for what he gave.
- To live under the American constitution is the greatest political privilege that was ever accorded to the human race.
- Don't expect to build up the weak by pulling down the strong.

- Four-fifths of all our troubles would disappear, if we would only sit down and keep still.

Franklin D. Roosevelt (1882–1945) was the 32nd president (1933–1945). He was elected to four terms in office and is the only president to have served more than two terms. He was a central figure of the twentieth century, during a time of worldwide economic crisis and world war.

An inscription on the new WW II memorial in Washington DC cites President Franklin Roosevelt's famous "day of Infamy" quotation about the attack of the Japanese on Pearl Harbor in 1941, but some say it leaves out the phrase "So help us God." The phrase was in a later part of the speech and not in this portion. Read on.

The inscription on the memorial reads:

> DECEMBER 7, 1941, A DATE WHICH WILL LIVE IN INFAMY ... NO MATTER HOW LONG IT MAY TAKE US TO OVERCOME THIS PREMEDITATED INVASION, THE AMERICAN PEOPLE IN THEIR RIGHTEOUS MIGHT, WILL WIN THROUGH TO ABSOLUTE VICTORY.

The inscription was derived from the following words of the first phrase:

> Yesterday, December 7, 1941—a date which will live in infamy—the United States of America was suddenly and deliberately attacked by naval and air forces of the Empire of Japan.

The inscription is condensed from the first phrase, then jumps down several paragraphs and draws a sentence from a portion of the speech that does not have any connection to the expression "So help us God." That phrase is near the end of the speech in a paragraph that says, "With confidence in our armed forces—with the unbounded determination of our people—we will gain the inevitable triumph—so help us God."

The next and final phrase was: "I ask that the Congress declare that since the unprovoked and dastardly attack by Japan on Sunday, December seventh, 1941, a state of war has existed between the United States and the Japanese Empire."

- The right thing to do never requires any subterfuge; it is always simple and direct.
- No person has ever been rewarded for what he received. Honor has been the reward for what he gave.
- To live under the American constitution is the greatest political privilege that was ever accorded to the human race.
- Physical strength can never permanently withstand the impact of spiritual force.
- Rules are not necessarily sacred, principles are.
- The only thing we have to fear is fear itself.

Harry S. Truman *(1884–1972)* was the 33rd president (1945–1953).

- In reading the lives of great men, I found that the first victory they won was over themselves: self-discipline with all of them came first.
- A politician is a man who understands government. A statesman is a politician who's been dead for fifteen years.
- My choice early in life was either to be a piano player in a whorehouse or a politician. And to tell you the truth, there's hardly any difference.
- Suppose you were an idiot. And suppose you were a Republican. But I repeat myself.
- Having found the bomb, we have used it. We have used it against those who attacked us without warning at Pearl Harbor, against those who have starved and beaten and executed American prisoners of war, against those who have abandoned all pretense of obeying international laws of warfare. We have used it in order to save the lives of thousands and thousands of young Americans. We will continue to use it until we completely destroy Japan's

power to make war. Only a Japanese surrender will stop us.

- When you have to deal with a beast, you have to treat him as a beast. It is most regrettable but nevertheless true.

Dwight David Eisenhower (1890–1969) was supreme commander of the Allied forces in Europe and 34th president (1953–1961). His family emigrated from Karlsbrunn (Saarland),Germany, to Lancaster PA in 1741.

- In preparing for battle, I have always found that plans are useless, but planning is indispensable.
- Things are more like they are now, than they have ever been before.

John F. Kennedy (1917–1963) was the 35th president serving from 1961 until his assassination in 1963. He is the youngest man and the only practicing Roman Catholic to have been elected president. To date, he is the only president to have won a Pulitzer Prize. Events during his administration include the Cuban Missile Crisis, the building of the Berlin Wall, the space race, the American Civil Rights movement, and the early phases of the Vietnam War.

- And so, my fellow Americans, ask not what your country can do for you; ask what you can do for your country.
- Change is the law of life. And those who look only to the past or present are certain to miss the future.

Ronald Reagan (1911–2004) was the 40th president of the United States (1981–1989) and the 33rd governor of California (1967–1975). He was born in Illinois and moved to California in the 1930s, where he became an actor, president of the Screen Actors Guild, and a spokesman for General Electric. In 1994, the former president disclosed that he had been diagnosed with Alzheimer's disease. He died ten years later at the age of ninety-three and ranks highly in approval rating among former presidents.

- It's true that hard work never killed anybody, but I figured, why take the chance?

- To sit back hoping that someday, someway, someone will make things right is to go on feeding the crocodile, hoping he will eat you last— but eat you he will.

Chapter 23:
Wise Sayings by an American Family— Mine

(This portion of Wise Sayings—for Your Thoughtful Consideration *is an example of things that could be written about any American family.)*

Walter Warwick Moore Jr (1923–) flew 30½ missions as a B-17 Flying Fortress bomber pilot with the Mighty Eighth Air Force during WW2. Shot down by German antiaircraft and was a prisoner of war for the duration. Military decorations include the Air Medal with four Oak Leaf Clusters. (The Air Medal was awarded to combat crew members after completing six combat missions over enemy territory. An Oak Leaf was awarded for each succeeding six missions.) Walter was a professional market researcher. After retiring he moved to Florida and became involved in several local and national societal organizations including genealogy.

- On a human-mind scale, a pint of misery has more emotional impact than a quart of happy.
- You don't have to be crazy to win in the stock market, but it helps.
- It's a breach of polite society to let the Wall Street bastards grind you down.
- My stock advice is free and worth every cent.
- You'll have better luck fishing for stocks on a rising tide.
- The stock market is a gambler's paradise: it is everywhere, and it is legal.
- Conceptual ideas and solutions that suddenly appear in your mind should be noted on paper at the moment of conception even if you are asleep.
- May the God force be with us and us with it.
- Play games with the odds in your favor—but not blackjack unless you are the dealer.

- The fun is collecting, not having—but having makes it possible to have more fun.
- Waiting time passes slowly.
- People who eat fast also think fast.
- Blue eyed people (like me) are smarter.
- It's the nature of things to cycle up and cycle down. Therefore, when things seem so bad they can't get any worse, look forward to tomorrow. You may be at the bottom of the cycle. Also, if things seem so good they can't get any better ... watch out!
- There is a natural tendency for live and inanimate things to cluster, i.e., bees swarm, birds flock, fish school, cows herd, dogs pack, people group, geese gaggle, lions pride, and baboons congress. Inanimate objects such as cars and trucks cluster on the highway. Floating flotsam and jetsam cluster in the ocean.
- One of the best ways to appreciate freedom is to lose it.
- A lot of positive things naturally accrue to being number one in an industry or organization.
- Many of the quotes from 500 BC and later are still relevant. Based on the proverbs, fables, folk sayings, and quotations derived from the wisdom of the ages: Matters of the mind and heart (including sex) are virtually the same as always. The major differences are that we now have super toys such as computers and better mass education.
- Throughout the ages, civilization has been blessed with some extremely intelligent individuals. It's reasonable to assume that the proportion of extreme intellects will increase as we build on previous knowledge, population increases, and the size and intelligence of our super toys such as the computer grow. In a way of speaking, the world is turning faster and faster with increasing intelligence. It may be something like the story about the bird that flew faster and faster in tighter circles until he swallowed himself.
- Thought transference between individuals and spirits can happen without reference to words in any language. This is also referred to as "mental telepathy" and "mind reading."

- Everything is all right as long as everything is all right. Meaning one flaw can spoil it all. This is akin to the fact that a chain is no stronger than its weakest link.
- I'll never be hungry again.
- If you want to know what freedom means, ask a former prisoner of war.

Robert Mitchell Moore (1956–) was an assistant manager for a Scotts Miracle-Gro plant.

- The best solution to a complex problem is often the simplest solution.

Andrew Warwick Moore (1957–) is founder and half-owner of Moore-Infranco Group, a full-service medical advertising company in New York City.

- When two sailboats are sailing in the same direction, they are in a race, whether or not the other boat knows it. (And so it is on the sea of life in general even without a sailboat. It's akin to the so-called "rat race.")

Karen Louise Silveira (1965–) (also known as Mrs. Andy Moore) was a graduate with all A's from Pratt Institute in Brooklyn and is now a vice-president with Tiffany's of New York City.

- It makes no sense to get angry at anybody.

Margaret Moore Johnston (1927–1989) was a highly trained professional nurse.

- Don't ever let the little boy inside you get out.

Walter Warwick Moore Sr (1900–1979) was involved in citrus, cattle, truck farming, and fishing.

- I feel good enough to climb a ten-foot cactus with a bobcat under each arm.

- Some days you get the bear, and some days the bear gets you.
- You always have time to do the things you want to do.
- Strong medicine comes in small bottles. [He was 5 feet 6 inches tall.]
- True friendship is a two-way street.
- The good Lord does not hold time against you when you are fishing.

Impertus Victor Moore (1869–1960) is one of my proven guardian angels.

- "Wait" is what broke down the wagon.
- "Can't" never did anything.
- I don't care how high the airplane flies as long as I can keep one foot on the ground.
- To remove that speck in your eye, grab the upper eyelash, pull outward, down, and release. Do it thrice.

Alice Mitchell Moore (1925–1988) was my wife for forty-six years and mother of my two sons and grandmother of four.

- There should be a third sex so women could have a choice.

William Victor Moore (1925–) is a combat veteran. He fought in Italy during WW2. His military decorations included a Bronze Star. (When awarded for bravery, it is the fourth highest combat award of the US Armed Forces. Bill helped retrieve a wounded buddy from an open field being strafed by enemy rifle fire.) Note: Only one of every fifteen soldiers during WW2 was a combat soldier. The others were support troops. Bill worked for Procter & Gamble.

- It's okay to disagree but not to be disagreeable.

Frank Johnston (1930–2009) was a psychiatrist, smart family doctor, and brother-in-law.

- In reference to a person who had just been diagnosed as

having lung cancer and restricted by her children from driving her car: "Tell them to let that woman do whatever the hell she wants, whenever the hell she wants, wherever the hell she wants—what, when, where, and have at it for the rest of her life."

- The world is an insane asylum, and some of us have walk-privileges sometimes. In other words, we all are crazy in various degrees at various times.

Alice Barrow Wojcinski (1926–)

- You can't catch no possums with your dogs tied.

William Henry Byrd (1869–1944), my maternal grandfather, was a woods rider for turpentine still companies.

- Little boys are made of nails and snails and puppydog tails. Little girls are made of sugar and spice and everything nice.
- If you lift a newborn bull calf over a fence and repeat it every day for a year or two, you will then will be able to lift a full-grown bull over the fence.

Virginia Bragg McCuen (1925–)

- Dear Walter:

  I have become a little older since I saw you last and a few changes have come into my life since then. Frankly, I have become quite a frivolous old gal. I am seeing five gentlemen every day. As soon as I wake up, Will Power helps me get out of bed; then I go see John. Then Charlie Horse comes along. And when he is here he takes a lot of my time. When he leaves, Arthur Ritis shows up and stays the rest of the day. He doesn't like to stay in one place very long, so he takes me from joint to joint. After such a busy day, I am tired and go to bed with Ben Gay. What a life!

  Love you, Cuzin Jiggs

Connie Moore *(1927–2007) was very actively involved in social work.*

- Fish and company begin to smell after three days.

Turner Brothers, Eugene *(1924–) **and Phillip** (1932–) are a tribute to American ingenuity and entrepreneurship. They specialize in citrus, cattle, and watermelons involving more than 12,000 acres of pasture with 4,000 head of Brangus cattle and about 5,000 acres of citrus. Gene served in the Army Air Corps during WW2. Phil was in the infantry during the Vietnam War.*

A verse framed and displayed prominently in Gene Turner's real estate office in downtown Arcadia sums up their shared philosophy. Titled "never stop working," it reads:

- If you are poor—work.
- If you are rich—continue to work
- If you are happy—keep right on working. Idleness gives you room for doubts and fears.
- If disappointments come—work
- If sorrow overwhelms you and loved ones seem untrue—work
- When dreams are shattered and hope seems dead—work
- Work as if your life was in peril, for it really is
- Whatever happens or matters—Work faithfully—work with faith
- Work is the greatest material remedy available.
- Work will cure both mental and physical afflictions.
- Work until *you feel you can work no more—then work a little more.*

Agnes Byrd Moore *(1903–1991), my mother, proved by her disposition that people can overcome obstacles in life in spite of being born without a silver spoon in their mouth. First, she was born prematurely—probably 6½ months and very tiny (1 or 1½ pounds)—over one hundred years ago. Her early arrival was probably not as much a surprise as her survival. Before age six and on her first day at school she determined to be a schoolteacher and never changed her mind. She played "make-*

believe schoolteacher" by arranging sticks in the ground and talking to them as if they were her students.

She suffered a great emotional loss at age sixteen when her mother died. Within a month or two the family moved to the Popash area, six miles from Wauchula, Florida. Some schools at the time consisted of one room with one teacher. Popash Elementary had three teachers. The first-grade teacher resigned, and Agnes got the job. She was sixteen, maybe seventeen years old at the time. She supported herself and her younger sister, Nadine. She continued teaching over a period of fifty years, mainly sixth grade, but also served as principal at Popash. While teaching, she received her high school diploma in Hardee County and a BS degree in elementary education from Florida Southern University in Lakeland. She was selected as teacher of the year in Hardee County during the early sixties and was later nominated for Florida teacher of the year. When she was in her late seventies, she commented that she wished she could be teaching today.

About the only thing Agnes could not conquer was fear of driving a car. Several of us tried to teach her, but she always panicked. We never understood why, but now we do. About six weeks after her mother died, the family decided to relocate from Pelham, Georgia, to south central Florida. There were six in the car. They were on a dirt road with deep ruts in an isolated part of the country south of Tallahassee. It was raining. The person driving at the time had very little experience. The car overturned and slid over an embankment, and Agnes was pinned under the car for an hour or so while they tried to figure out what to do. This event happened under primitive conditions. No doctors and no ambulances or wreckers came to the rescue. In those days you did what you could with what you had and moved on. However, Agnes had had a traumatic experience she would never forget. Traumatic experiences that last in the mind forever were recognized as a military problem long ago and called battle fatigue in WW2, shell shock in WW1, and soldier's heart during the Civil War. It was largely disregarded for decades until the Vietnam War. Now, since 1980, PTSD has been a diagnosable anxiety disorder. PTSD is why Agnes could never overcome her fear of driving a car. In later years, Agnes wrote a story about an experience she had before the wreck, Agnes wrote the following tale:

Margaret Wilson Byrd (1879–1920), my mother, was sick in bed with TB (tuberculosis) and just wasting away. Doctors had done all they could do. A friend asked her to try some Christian Science, which she did. I sat by my mother's bedside and read Christian Science aloud to her for hours at a time. Although Christian Science today is considered a cult, there are some good things about it when rightly understood. Some wrong conclusions have been made about it. Remember, I was reading this at the age of sixteen. Years later, and even now, I can see some of the principles of Christian Science being taught by other churches and by some doctors. For instance, some doctors may tell you that many of their patients have nothing wrong with them, but they think they have. Some doctors even agree one can think himself into having a certain disease. Also, the doctors have to treat some patients mentally before they can do anything for them physically. Christian Science teaches mind over *matter.*

Sookie Moore (1997–), my fourteen-year-old Shih Tzu, says: "Don't forget your dog. We animals can have PTSD too. For example: I licked a hot fry pan when I was a little puppy. Now I back off whenever I see a skillet."

Bill and Jim Moore (1956–), my nephews, are both captains on transcontinental flights in a Boeing 777, the biggest commercial jets, which fly five hundred miles per hour to faraway places like Buenos Aires, Tokyo, London, Dublin, Cape Town, Athens, Rome, Paris, Prague, and Milan. The irony of it all is that they can almost touch the unreachable star, and they get paid for doing it.

> *Bill: Make my day: Be one of my two hundred or more passengers on Delta Airlines out of Atlanta.*
> *Jim: Make my day: Be one of my two hundred or more passengers on American Airlines out of Dallas.*
> *Jim: Speed is life. There is no corner too square, and I would rather die than look bad.*

Richard Otis Powell (1931–) sensed from his early life that he was destined to be a teacher. In his senior year in high school he told his dad that he wanted to go to college. His dad told him he was unable to help. So he found that Georgia Tech had a co-op program which allowed students to attend school half-time and work in industry half-time. However, after his first year he was called to active duty in the naval reserves for two years, but then he was able to use the GI Bill to go to school full time.

After graduation, fortune smiled again, and he was hired by Tulane to teach full time and to work on his master's degree with free tuition. Ten years later he decided to go for his doctorate at the University of Hawaii. He and his wife Gloria bought a house within a week of arriving, which saved thousands of dollars because he was exempt from paying higher costing out-of-state tuition. They had saved enough that they could pay their own way—but just barely. At the end of the first semester he was offered a full-time job on the faculty and allowed to work full time on his doctorate. It worked out so well that their financial situation changed from eating macaroni and cheese to eating steaks in the finest restaurants.

They gave up a good job and returned to New Orleans. Doctor Powell began teaching engineering courses full time at Tulane University and doing consulting work on the side. He worked on several of the skyscrapers now dotting the New Orleans skyline, most notably the Plaza Tower. This building was built before the World Trade Center in New York City, whose structural design was based on the Plaza Tower technique. Doctor Powell's consulting work extended to other cities and other states. He traveled to these jobs in his private airplane. Dick also was a golfer until he retired to the renowned golf country near Pinehurst, NC. He is now teaching an engineering course at a local college. So, after forty-one years of full-time teaching and eighty years of experience, he is still at it.

- If you want something—go for it! It can't happen if you don't try.
- Things have a way of working out.
- I have found that when you have a plan and you look hard enough, somehow the answers show up, and opportunities

show up in such a way that one has to believe in divine help.

Donald Dean Buchanan (1922–2005). Buck enlisted in the Army Air Corps in 1941 and later was assigned to the 378th Technical Squadron of the Eighth Air Force in England. He codesigned and converted a wrecked P51 fighter into a tandem two-seater aircraft. It was the only one in Europe during World War II. He joined NASA (National Aeronautics and Space Administration) when it was formed in 1960. He had a key role in the design of the launch facilities for the Apollo program. From 1967 until he retired in 1981 he was the Chief Design Engineer for NASA at Kennedy Space Center, FL. He received many awards for his contributions, notably NASA's Exceptional Service Medal (twice), the Distinguished Service Medal (NASA's highest award), and the Medal for Exceptional Engineering Achievement. In London, in 1969, he was awarded the Royal Automobile Club Diamond Jubilee Trophy, "the world's most prestigious transportation honor" for the design of the Crawler system used to move a mobile launcher with a fully assembled and checked-out lunar vehicle aboard from the Vehicle Assembly Building to the launch pads some 3½ to 4¼ miles away.

The crawler-transporter weighs about six million pounds and carries a load of approximately 12 million pounds. It travels at speeds up to one mile per hour. Since the crawler-transporter became operational in 1966, they have been used for all vehicles launched from Kennedy Space Center.

- They didn't know how to spell my name. [Referring to a brick with names of key NASA personnel on a walkway.]

Paul Eugene Buchanan (1929–1993). The Paul E. Buchanan award is named for second cousin Paul E. Buchanan who served for thirty years as the Director of Architectural Research at Colonial Williamsburg Foundation. Buchanan set the standard for architectural fieldwork in America. The Paul E. Buchanan award is presented annually by the Vernacular Architects Foundation to architects as recognition for their value.

Karen Lee Moore (1942–)

- We have long been taught to only color inside the lines. Breaking this rule is not only permissible but highly recommended.
- If in doubt, don't, don't, don't.

Nina Powell Spivey (1939–) was an office manager in charge of a group of court reporters.

- No one can make me mad unless I let them.

Nancy Kay Powell Lovelace (1942–) is a retired senior vice president and corporate communications manager of Wachovia Corporation of Winston-Salem, NC.

- Forward hindsight is the best way to predict the future because history has a way of repeating itself.

Otis Powell (1901–1972) was noted for having an easygoing, winning personality that made everybody like him instantly if they didn't already know him. Dogs loved him too. His gifted hobby was training bird dogs and hunting quail. He had a reputation for being good at both. It has been said that a dog's sense of smell is 400 times greater than that of humans. Quail hunting involves utilizing this knack. The dogs are turned loose in quail country and watched while they seek the odor of a quail trail that will lead them to a covey of usually about fifteen to twenty birds on the first flush. Quails leave trails because they are ground travelers. When they are located, the dog sets the covey by somehow mesmerizing them in their hiding place until the hunter arrives with a cocked 12-gauge shotgun. Then the birds are flushed. All birds rise at the same instant; their wings make a loud sudden noise that is intended to startle any predators. Each hunter may get one to three before the birds are out of gun range. The dogs are trained to fetch the dropped birds

- Never point a gun at a man unless you intend to shoot him. Never shoot a man unless you intend to kill him.

Admiral Richard Evelyn Byrd Jr (1888–1957) was born in Virginia and was a descendant of a high society order of early Virginians with class, called "FFV—First Families of Virginia." He graduated from the US Naval Academy and specialized in feats of exploration including five expeditions to Antarctica. On his second expedition, in 1934, Byrd spent five winter months alone operating a meteorological station. His fourth expedition was massive and involved over 4,000 personnel who mapped an area half the size of the United States. In all, he was awarded twenty-two citations and special commendations plus three ticker-tape parades. And he was present at the Japanese surrender. His ancestors included planter John Rolfe and his wife Pocahontas. He was the brother of Virginia Governor and US Senator Harry F. Byrd.

Partial List of Medals Awarded to Rear Admiral Richard E. Byrd, USN:

> Medal of Honor (1926) (Rare Tiffany Cross version)
> Navy Cross
> Navy Distinguished Service Medal with Gold Star
> Legion of Merit with Gold Star
> Distinguished Flying Cross (1926)
> Navy Commendation Medal
> Victory Medal (1918)
> Byrd Antarctic Expedition Medal (1928–1930)
> Second Byrd Antarctic Expedition Medal (1933–1935)
> US Antarctic Expedition (1939–1941)
> World War Two Victory Medal (1945)

- Give wind and tide a chance to change.
- Half the confusion in the world comes from not knowing how little we need.
- Few men during their lifetime come anywhere near exhausting the resources dwelling within them. There are deep wells of strength that are never used.
- No woman has ever stepped on Little America ... and we have found it to be the most silent and peaceful place in the world.

Robert Wallie Powell (1961–), summa cum laude lawyer who chose to teach rather than practice.

- I'd rather be an hour early than a second late.

Richard Powell-Moulter (1953–) had a career with the US Air Force, providing whatever technology and consultation was needed for whatever communications job. He also is the genealogist for the Byrd family. His records go back to the 1500s.

- When you're in the service of your fellow beings, you are only in the service of your God.

Karen Jane May (1957–) (also known as Mrs. Bob Moore) is an accountant at the University of Delaware.

- What lies behind us and what lies before us are tiny matters compared with what lies within us.

Chapter 24:
Universal Laws, Principles, and Rules

Universal laws (sometimes referred to as spiritual or cosmic laws) are laws whose content is set by nature. They govern the universe. They are basic principles of life and have been around since creation. They are the laws of the Divine Universe. They apply to everyone, everywhere. They cannot be changed. They cannot be broken.

All or most of nature's laws have been identified and widely accepted as laws. There are many "near-laws" that are close but not widely accepted. They are identified variously as "theories, rules, doctrines, quotations, legends, codes, sayings, and street gospel. This category can be individually accepted, dismissed, or rejected, but widely accepted universal laws are facts.

Natural laws of the universe are discussed below. Note that these are grouped broadly into major subject matters.

THE UNIVERSAL LAW OF ATTRACTION AND VIBRATION

This is the most powerful combination law in the universe. It is simple in concept. The actual definition varies greatly. The simplest definition of this law is "like attracts like, and opposites repel." Other interpretations include:

- All forms of matter and energy are attracted to that which is of a like vibration.
- You are a living magnet.
- Energy attracts like energy.
- Everything draws to itself that which is like itself.

Here are some ways the Law of Attraction is expressed:

- Birds of a feather flock together.
- Like attracts like: opposites repel.
- Whatever you want wants you.
- What you sow, you reap.

- What comes around goes around.
- Fish school, sheep flock, cows herd, bees swarm, dogs pack …

The Law of Vibration

According to this law, everything vibrates, nothing rests. This phenomenon is closely allied with the law of attraction. Vibrations are the essence of the law of attraction. All things vibrate but at varying frequencies. Those things with harmonious frequencies attract each other. Vibrations are often referred to as "vibes." Vibrations can have a positive, neutral, or negative effect and may partially explain a cause or a result of love and friendly relations and criminal activity. This law and the conjoining Law of Attraction also may help explain the clustering tendency of people, animals, and inanimate objects

THE LAW OF CAUSE AND EFFECT

- Whatever goes around comes around. Whatever you send into the universe comes back. So say good things to everyone.

Isaac Newton (1643–1727) was an English physicist, mathematician, astronomer natural philosopher, and alchemist, regarded by many as the greatest scientist in the history of mankind. His claim to fame is based on his laws of motion and universal gravitation.

- For every action there is an equal and opposite reaction.
- The behavior of all objects can be described by saying that objects tend to "keep on doing what they're doing" (unless they are acted upon by an unbalanced force).
- Acceleration is produced when a force acts on a mass. The greater the mass (of the object being accelerated), the greater the amount of force needed (to accelerate the object).

THE LAW OF USE

- Basically, it's use it or lose it.
- The possession of knowledge unless manifested by an expression in action is a foolish thing. Wealth, like knowledge, is intended for use. In other words, anytime

the supreme commander gives you something extra like money, power, exceptional ability to do things, deep insight, special revelations, etc., he holds you accountable for what you do with it. Problem is, opportunity is often difficult to recognize. It rarely beckons with bugles and billboards.

The Law of Thinking

According to Clark Pasag, thought is a form of energy. It is a substance or an actual force, despite the fact that it is invisible. It is like electricity. He says it is quicker than the speed of light (which is the fastest form of energy and travels at a speed of 186,000 miles per second). Thoughts are power, and power will always produce an effect. A book on *The Power of Intention* by Dr. Wayne W. Dyer says intention is a force in the universe, and everything and everyone is connected to this invisible force. Other books have been written on the power of positive thinking. Most of the soothsayers agree that you are what you think. If that is so, then the physical body is just a transporter for the thinking mind.

The Law of Relativity

Nothing is good or bad, big or small ... until you relate it to something. Try relating your situation to something much worse, and yours will look good.

Albert Einstein (1879–1955), was a German-born American physicist who developed the special and general theories of relativity. He won the Nobel Prize for physics in 1921.

- Put your hand on a hot stove for a minute, and it seems like an hour. Sit with a pretty girl for an hour, and it seems like a minute. That's relativity.

LAWS OF THERMODYNAMICS

The laws of thermodynamics, in principle, describe the specifics for the transport of heat and work in thermodynamic processes. Since their conception (circa 1824), however, these laws have become some of the most important in all of physics and other branches of science connected to thermodynamics.

If two thermodynamic systems are each in thermal equilibrium with a third, then they are in thermal equilibrium with each other. In any process, the total energy of a closed system (e.g. the universe) remains the same. More simply, the law states that energy cannot be created or destroyed, just transformed to another form of energy.

The entropy (chaos) of an isolated system not in equilibrium will tend to increase over time, approaching a maximum value at equilibrium. In a simple manner, the law states that "energy systems have a tendency to increase their entropy rather than decrease it." Likewise, solid crystals, the most organized form of matter, have low entropy values; and gases, which are highly disorganized, have high entropy values.

Entropy is:

Inevitable and steady deterioration of a system or society.

The tendency for all matter and energy in the universe to evolve toward a state of inert uniformity.

The tendency of all things including concepts to disintegrate or fall apart.

As temperature approaches absolute zero, the entropy (chaos rate) of a system approaches a constant minimum. In brief, this postulates that entropy is temperature dependent and leads to the formulation of the idea of absolute zero. (Absolute zero is the lowest possible temperature where nothing could be colder, and no heat energy remains in a substance.)

The Law of Rhythm in Action

Things cycle up, and things cycle down. Usually, the more we fight an adverse situation, the tighter the adverse forces hold on. It's easier to float downstream than to fight against the current. This doesn't mean that you just let things happen indiscriminately in your life. Rather, you adjust to the condition as much as possible and wait for the positive flow in the cycle. Also, when you feel things can't get any worse, look to tomorrow because they have to be better.

The Law of Gender

One of nature's laws is that life has to start with a seed and requires a gestation or incubation period. Similarly, ideas are spiritual seeds and fall in the same requirement that they also require time to incubate. They will hatch sooner or later if and when it's the right time. As said by Victor-Marie Hugo "All the forces in the world are not as powerful as an idea whose time has come."

The Law of Balance

All things seek a natural state of balance and equilibrium. Water is a good example.

The Law of Love

There is no opposite pole to love, only distortions of the concept, much as there is no source of darkness, just light and things that block the light.

Laws of Life for an Educated Person in Today's Culture

- kindness and protection of the young
- knowledge of our ancestors, our heritage, and our respect for the elderly
- generosity to the poor
- good counsel to friends
- forbearance with enemies
- indifference to fools
- respect for the learned

Murphy's Original Three Laws

1. If anything can possibly go wrong, it will.
2. Left to themselves, things invariably go from "bad" to "worse."
3. Nature always finds the hidden flaw.

Some of the corollaries to Murphy's Three Laws

- No matter how hard you try, you can't push a string.
- Nothing is impossible for the man who doesn't have to do it himself.
- Rule of Accuracy: When working toward the solution of a problem, it always helps if you know the answer.

- Corollary: Provided, of course, that you know there is a problem.
- Nothing is as easy as it looks.
- Everything takes longer than you think.
- Everything takes longer than it takes.
- If anything simply cannot go wrong, it will anyway.
- Whenever you set out to do something, something else must be done first.
- A falling object will always land where it can do the most damage.
- No good deed goes unpunished.
- Anything good in life is either illegal, immoral, or fattening.
- If in a particular circumstance Murphy's laws don't apply, then something else must be wrong.
- If Murphy's law is right, then it will go wrong.
- Inside every large problem is a small problem struggling to get out.
- A complex system that works is invariably found to have evolved from a simple system that works.
- The specialist learns more and more about less and less until finally, he knows everything about nothing; whereas the generalist learns less and less about more and more until, finally, he knows nothing about everything.
- After all is said and done, a hell of a lot more is said than done.
- If you can't understand it, it is intuitively obvious.
- When all else fails, read the instructions.
- It is never wise to let a piece of electronic equipment know that you are in a hurry.
- An expert will always state the obvious.
- You can get *anywhere* in ten minutes if you go fast enough.
- A great many problems do not have accurate answers but do have approximate answers, from which sensible decisions can be made.
- In any household, junk accumulates to fill the space available for its storage.
- It's better to be rich and healthy than poor and sick.

- Every revolutionary idea—in science, politics, art, or whatever—evokes three stages of reaction. They may be summed up by three phrases:
  1. "It is completely impossible—don't waste my time."
  2. "It is possible, but it is not worth doing."
  3. "I said it was a good idea all along."
- If on an actuarial basis there is a 50–50 chance that something will go wrong, it will go wrong nine times out of ten.
- The most ominous words for those using computers: "Daddy, what does 'Now formatting drive C' mean?"
- Nothing is so good as it seems beforehand.
- The other line moves faster.
- You never run out of things that can go wrong.
- The man shalt not win the argument he started.
- The man shalt not win the argument he didn't start.
- If a man won an argument, it was just in his head.
- If you know you are correct, then you aren't.
- You are not young enough to know it all.
- If a man speaks deep in the forest and there is no woman to hear him, is he still wrong?

THE PARETO PRINCIPLE

Joseph M. Juran (1904–2008) was a twentieth-century management consultant who is principally remembered as an evangelist for quality and quality management, writing several influential books on those subjects.

- **The Pareto principle** (also known as the 80-20 rule, the law of the vital few and the trivial many) states that, for many events, 80 percent of the effects come from 20 percent of the causes. Business management thinker Joseph M. Juran suggested the principle and named it after Italian economist Vilfredo Pareto, who observed that 80 percent of income in Italy went to 20 percent of the population. It is a common rule of thumb in business; e.g., "80 percent of your sales come from 20 percent of your clients."
- It is worthy of note that some applications of the Pareto

163

principle appeal to a pseudoscientific "law of nature" to bolster nonquantifiable or nonverifiable assertions that are "painted with a broad brush." The fact that hedges like the 90/10, 70/30, and 95/5 "rules" exist is sufficient evidence of the nonexactness of the Pareto principle. On the other hand, there is adequate evidence that "clumping" of factors does occur in most phenomena.

Leonardo Bonacci (1170–1240 Best est.) was considered a great genius in mathematics. He developed a number theory that relates to nature's laws and named it after himself.

- **Fibonacci Numbers** consist of spectacular ratios that are found everywhere in nature, such as flower petal counts, suspension bridges, spider webs, dripping taps, and such. Mathematically, the first two numbers are 0 and 1, and each subsequent number is the sum of the previous two, i.e, 0, 1, 1, 2, 3, 5, 8, 13, 21—. These numbers can be parlayed into various ratios, such as Pareto's principal and his 80–20 rule, and graphically illustrated.

The Three-to-Five, Three-to-Five Rule
- If you want to lock information into long-term memory, you'll need to review it for three to five times a day for three to five days.

A MEMORY RULE
- Don't try to memorize words; visualize them. Microphone stands for Mike, Toilet seat for john, Magic marker for Mark, Hot dog for Frank, Baltimore for Waltermoore.

Occam's Razor is a principle attributed to the fourteenth-century logician and Franciscan friar William of Ockham. Ockham was the village in the English County of Surrey where he was born.

The principle goes back at least as far as Aristotle, who wrote, "Nature operates in the shortest way possible."

KISS is a modern way of expressing the principle. KISS is an acronym for "Keep It Simple, Stupid."

The final word is of unknown origin, although the concept is often attributed to Einstein who wrote, "Everything should be made as simple as possible but not simpler."

Occam's Razor is often expressed as the law of parsimony, the law of economy, the law of succinctness, or the law of simplicity. It also is referred to as a principle or a rule and not as one of nature's laws.

An example: The Americans reportedly spent a ton of money developing, or trying to develop, a pen that would write in outer space. The Russians used a pencil.

The Law of Polarity or the Law of Opposites recognizes that there are "two sides to everything" such as north pole – south pole, positive – negative, hot – cold, love – hate. The law says everything has an opposite that is equal. Then there are perceptions of what is good or bad that may be lop-sided. Explained in the words of an un-named Jewish Mother (a classification of women recognized as being smart and always right) "there is nothing so good that there is not some bad associated with it and nothing so bad that there is not some good associated with it". Another explanation is that nothing is good or bad except that thinking makes it so. If the Law of Polarity, with some help from the Law of Balance works, it would mean that when something goes wrong, something else will come along eventually to restore the right balance. If something you considered bad happens in your life, there has to be a correction sooner or later that may not be evident at the time. Also, it is a matter of thinking. If you think something is bad, think about the merits from the opposite view point and it will be positive. The law applies to good and bad perceptions about situations and people.

The Akashi Records is a concept originated by Sanskrit speaking people in ancient India. (Sanskrit is one of twenty-two languages still spoken in in various parts of India). Believers of the Akashi concept say all the thoughts and events that have ever occurred is recorded in an astral non-physical plane somewhere up there in the sky. As far-advanced as the concept may seem, (from 2000 years ago) it may be only a matter of time before easy access to the records are achieved if such records actually exist. Some psychics, such as Edgar Cayce (See page 125) and others claim to have accessed the records through self-induced hypnotic trances. The theory is loaded with religious insinuations. Nicholas Zaharis, a Greek-oriented self-taught psychic may have made a clairvoyant statement when he stated that religion is still in its infancy. (See page 35). Vast improvements in computerized memory systems may be narrowing the information gap between human and divine knowledge. Whatever, it is difficult to imagine what the changes in human knowledge and behavior will be like in the next fifty years and beyond, and how we handle it.

Glossary

PG.	NAME	LIFESPAN	QUOTES
133	Adams, John	1735 - 1826	3
133	Adams, Samuel	1722 - 1803	1
36	Aesop	620 BC - 560 BC	2
82	Ah Those British		1
66	Al ahnaf, Abbas Lbn	750 - 809	1
34	Albom, Mitch	1958 -	1
101	Alfred Lord Tenneyson	1809 - 1892	1
165	Alkasic Records		
61	Allen, Brant	1940 -	18
47	Allen, James	1864 - 1912	1
57	Allen, Woody	1935 -	1
4	Anderson, Michael P.	1959 - 2003	1
35	Anonymous Prayer		1
97	Anonymous Proverbs		4
121	Aragon, Louis	1897 - 1982	1
52	Aristotle	384 - 322BC	2
64	Aristotle	384BC - 322BC	8
71	Ash, Mary Kay	1918 - 2001	1
8	Asimov, Issac	1920 - 1992	3
5	Aurelius, Marcus	121 - 180	1
52	Ball, Lucille	1911 - 1989	1
3	Banister, Roger	1929	1
26	Barkier, Harriet	1858 -1912	1
89	Barkley, Charles	1963 -	1
111	Barry, Dave	1947 -	1
11	Baruch, Bernard	1870 - 1965	4
38	Battista, O. A.	1917 -1995	11
19	Beethoven, Ludwig van	1770 - 1827	1

112	Benchly, Robert	1889 - 1945	1
51	Benny, Jack	1894 - 1974	1
52	Berle, Milton	1908 - 2002	1
90	Berra, Yogi	1925 -	14
37	Bible		3
112	Bierce, Ambrose	1842 - 1914	1
83	Billings, Josh	1818 - 1885	7
94	Black, Shirley Temple	1928 -	1
164	Bonacci, Leonardo	1170 - 1240	1
124	Bonaparte, Napoleon	1769 - 1821	1
32	Born, Max	1882 - 1970	1
7	Bowden, Bobby	1929 -	2
121	Bradley, Bill	1953 -	1
121	Bradley, Ed	1941 - 2006	1
72	Brett, Regina	1956 -	45
83	Brigham, Richard	1939Est	1
115	Bright, John	1811 - 1889	1
78	Bronte,, Charlotte	1816 - 1855	2
76	Brothers, Joyce	1925	1
30	Brown, H. Jackson Jr.	1948	12
152	Buchanan, Donald Dean	1922 - 2005	6
152	Buchanan, Paul Eugene	1929 - 1993	2
86	Buffett, Jimmy	1946 -	3
70	Buffett, Warren	1930 -	3
134	Burke, Edmond	1727 - 1797	1
51	Burns, George	1896 - 1996	3
150	Byrd ,Margaret Wilson	1879 - 1920	1
154	Byrd, Adm. Richard E. Jr.	1888 - 1957	1
147	Byrd, William Henry	1869 - 1944	2
12	Caesar, Julius	100BC - 44BC	1
96	Camus, Albert	1913 - 1960	2
56	Carnegie, Andrew	1835 - 1919.	2
6	Carniegie, Dale.	1888 -1955	4
47	Carver, George Washington	1864 - 1943	1

27	Cathy, Samuel Truett	1921 -	2
125	Cayce, Edgar	1887 - 1945	10
1	Cervantes,de Miguel	1547 -1616	7
35	Chardin, Pierre Teilhard de	1881 -1955	4
8	Chesterton, C.K.	1874 - 1936	2
19	Chopin, Frederick	1810 - 1849	1
78	Chopin, Kate	1851 - 1904	1
33	Christ, Jesus		1
27	Churchill, Sir Winston	1874 - 1965	4
88	Churchill, Sir Winston	1874 - 1965	2
115	Churchill, Winston	1874 - 1965	1
94	Churchill, Winston	1874 - 1965	1
115	Cobb, Irving S.	1876 - 1944	1
128	Collier, Robert	1885 - 1950	1
47	Coloridge, Taylor	1772 -1834	1
75	Colton, Caleb	1780 - 1832	1
130	Confucius	551BC - 479BC	11
46	Congreve, William	1670 - 1729	1
8	Conwell, Russell H.	1843 - 1925	1
137	Coolidge, Calvin	1872 - 1933	5
63	Cousins, Norman	1915 - 1990	3
119	Covey, Steven	1932 -	1
66	Cozzens, James Gould	1903 -1978	1
105	Crosby, Bing	1903 - 1977	12
82	Crow, Bill	1923 -	1
16	da Vinci, Leonnardo	1452 -1519	9
26	Dali, Salvador	1904 -1989	3
130	Dalton, Kevlin	Abt 1988	1
130	Dalton, Kevlin	Abt 1988	1
93	Davies, Robertson	1913 - 1995	1
51	Davis, Bette	1908 - 1989	1
5	Demostehenes	384BC -322BC	4
88	DeSaint, Antoine Exupery	1893 - 1986	1
67	Descartes, Rene	1596 - 1650	1

83	Diefenbaker, John G.	1895 -1979	1
29	Disney, Walt	1901 - 1966	15
36	Disrali, Benjamin	1804 -1881	1
83	Doctor's Gospel		1
106	Doris Day	1922 -	6
77	Dr. Seuss		4
41	Drucker, Peter	1909 - 2005	2
60	du Pont, Henry A.	1838 - 1926	1
128	Durant, Will	1885 - 1981	1
91	Durante, Jimmy	1893 - 1980	8
60	Dylan, Bob	1941 -	1
81	Earhart, Amelia	1897 - 1939	1
131	Eastman, Charles Alexander	1858 - 1939	1
93	Ecclesiastes 9.11 NIV		1
10	Edison, Thomas	1847 - 1931	4
101	Ehrmann, Max	1872 - 1945	1
62	Einstein, Albert	1879 - 1955	5
140	Eisenhower, Dwight David	1890 - 1969	2
7	Ellington, Duke	1899 -1974	1
122	Emerson, Ralph Waldo	1803 - 1882	7
31	Euripides	ca 480BC- 405BC	8
76	Ewing, David	1955 -	2
96	Farbar, Barry	1930 -	1
82	Feather, William	1889 - 1981	8
25	Fine, Paul A.	1935?	1
3	Forbes, Malcolm	1919 - 1990	3
112	Ford, Corey	1902 - 1969	1
41	Ford, Henry	1863 - 1947	9
37	Fosdick, Harry Emerson	1878 -1969	2
79	Frank. Anne	1929 - 1945	4
71	Frankl, Viktor	1905 - 1997	1
99	Franklin. Ben	1706 - 1790	8
81	Freud, Sigmund	1856 - 1939	1
90	Frost, Robert	1874 - 1963	5

3	Gandhi, Mahatna	1869 -1948	3
28	Gartner, Michael	1938 -	5
75	Gauss, Carl Friedrich	1777 - 1855	1
128	Gawain, Shakti	1948 -	5
95	German Proverb		1
60	Getty, J. Paul	1896 - 1996	1
96	Gibran, Kahlil	1883 -1931	1
99	Giovanni, Fra	1513 -	1
106	Glenn Miller	1904 - 1944	9
33	God		1
91	Goldwyn, Samuel	1879 - 1974	16
19	Gracian, Baltasar	1601 - 1658	2
45	Grayson, David	1964 -	4
65	Greeley, Horace	1811 - 1872	1
71	Greenleaf, Robert K.	1904 - 1990	2
112	Grizzard, Lewis	1946 -1994	2
13	Gross, Bill	1944 -	1
115	Hadas, Moses	1900 - 1966	1
4	Hagen, Walter	1892 - 1969	2
65	Halas, George	1895 1983	1
123	Hallowell, Dr. Edward	1035 - 2009	1
20	Hammarskjold, Dag	1905 - 1961	3
133	Hancock, John	1737 - 1793	2
119	Handy, Charles	1932 -	1
65	Harris, Sdney J.	1917 - 1986	1
63	Harvey, Paul	1918 -	1
89	Heinlein, Robert A.	1907 - 1988	9
111	Heinlein, Robert A.	1907 - 1988	1
6	Heinz, Teresa	1938 -	1
118	Hemmingway, Earnest	1899 - 1961	1
134	Henry, Patrick	1735 - 1799	2
95	Heraclitus	535 - 475 BC	1
112	Hill, Gene	1923 - 2005	2
118	Hill, Napoleon	1883 - 1970	2

117	History Channel		1
76	Hoffman, Hans	1880 - 1965	1
35	Holmes, Oliver Wendell	1809 - 1894	1
59	Hopkins, Tom	?	2
115	Hudson, Rex	?	1
21	Hugo, Victor-Marie	1802 -1885	3
45	Hugo, Victor-Marie	1802 - 1885	5
23	Huxley, Aldous	1894 -1963	1
4	Iacocca, Lee	1924 -	2
66	Inge, William Ralph	1860 - 1954	1
52	Investor's Business Daily		1
52	Jackson, Holbrook	1874 - 1948	1
38	James, William	1842 -1910	1
135	Jefferson, Thomas	1743 - 1826	6
21	Jemison, Mae	1956 -	2
88	John ?	?	1
146	Johnston, Frank	1930 - 2009	2
145	Johnston, Margaret Moore	1927 - 1989	2
19	Joyce, James	1882 - 1941	1
86	Judd, H. Stanley	1950 -	1
86	Judd, Stanley	1950 -	4
46	Jung, Carl	1875 - 1961	4
76	Kappa Sigma Fraternity		1
7	Kapuscinski, Ryszard	1932 -2007	1
61	Kass, Leon	1939 -	1
29	Keller, Helen	1880 - 1968	1
10	Keller. Jeffrey	1961 - 2010	1
140	Kennedy, John F.	1917 - 1963	3
48	King, Martin Luther	1929 - 1968	2
128	King, Stephen	1947 -	5
120	Koch, Richard	1950 -	1
59	Kruse, Shirley	1921 -	1
111	Landers, Ann	1918 - 2002	1

140	Reagan, Ronald	1911 - 2004	23
6	Reeves, Dan	1944 -	1
39	Reid, Dr. Ron	1924 -	2
53	Remember		3
127	Richards, Ann	1933- 2006	2
67	Road Side Church Sign		2
37	Robison, Diana	?	1
68	Rogers, Ginger	1911 -1995	1
64	Rogers, Kenny	1938 -	1
84	Rogers, Will	1879 - 1935	6
23	Rohn, Jim	1930 - 2009	6
58	Rooney, Andy	1919 - 2011	6
111	Rooney, Andy	1919 - 2011	1
67	Roosevelt, Eleanor	1884 - 1962	1
138	Roosevelt, Franklin D.	1882 - 1945	6
137	Roosevelt, Theodore	1858 - 1919	2
97	Rowling, J. K.	1965 -	1
41	Saint-Exupery, Antoine	1900 -1944	2
129	Santayana, Geoge S.	1863 -1952	2
69	Sched, Fred Jr.	?	2
65	Schickel, Richard	1933 -	1
70	Schlesinger, Arthur M.	1917 - 2007	1
76	Schuller, Robert	1926	1
85	Schultz, Charles	1922 - 2000	2
53	Schwartz, Jeremy	1971 -	2
34	Schwartz, Maurie	1916 - 1995	5
23	Schwarzkopf, Norman	1934 -	2
13	Schweitzer, Albert	1875 - 1965	2
59	Scott, Sir Walter	1771 - 1832	1
88	Scully, Vin	1927	1
20	Seneca	4BC -AD65	8
25	Shakespeare, William	1564 -1616	4
46	Shakespeare, William	1564 -1616	4
65	Shakespeare, William	1564 -1616	1

129	Shakespeare, William	1564 - 1616	1
87	Shaw, George Bernard	1856 - 1950	1
115	Shaw, George Bernard		7
94	Shay, R. E.	?	1
52	Sibelius, Jean	1865 - 1957	1
27	Sign on VA clinic wall		1
145	Silveria, Karen Louise	1965 -	1
29	Socrates	469BC - 399BC	6
32	Sophocles	C. 496 - 406 BC	14
65	Sophocles	C.496 - 406 BC	14
34	Spellman, Francis	1889 - 1967	1
153	Spivey, Nina Powell	1939 -	4
62	Steinbeck, John	1902 - 1968	1
120	Steinbeck, John	1902 - 1968	2
68	Stone, W. Clement	1902 - 2002	2
33	Street Gospel		5
57	Street Gospel		10
60	Street Gospel		4
66	Street Gospel		2
113	Street Gospel		4
39	Strode, Muriel	1875 -1930	2
55	Sugar, Alan	1947 -	1
89	Sutton, Willie	1901 - 1980	1
128	Swindoll, Charles (Chuck)	1934 -	1
117	Swing, Larry	?	1
62	Szent-Gyorgye, Albert	1893 - 1986	2
109	Ten Commandments		10
88	Tenneyson, Alfred Lord	1809 - 1892	10
39	Teresa, Mother	1910 - 1970	1
20	Thatcher, Margaret	1945 - 1990	4
118	Thomas, Danny	1912 - 1991	4
7	Thomas, Dave	1932 - 2002	1
81	Thompson, Bill	1925 Est	1
82	Thompson, Fred	1942 -	1

3	Thoreau, Henry David	1817 -1872	4
86	Thurber. James	1894 - 1961	4
11	Tocqueville, Alexis de	1805 - 1859	3
68	Tomlin, Lily	1939 -	3
100	Towne, Charles Hanson	1877 - 1949	1
14	Tracy, Brian	1944 -	15
139	Truman, Harry S.	1884 - 1972	15
119	Truth, Sojourner	1797 - 1883	1
47	Tsunetomo, Yamamoto	1659 - 1719	1
148	Turner Btothers, Eugene & Phil	1924 1932	11
85	Twain, Mark	1835 -1910	10
55	Unknown author		10
77	Vales, MG Luis Gonzalez		1
53	VEW Post 8696		1
24	VFW(Vets of Foreign Wars)		1
26	Virgil	70BCE-19BCE	1
22	Voltaire	1694 -1778	7
88	Wadsworth, Charles	1928	1
9	Waitley, Denis	1924 -	8
46	Wallenda, Karl	1905 - 1978	1
120	Walpole, Hugh	1884 - 1941	1
28	Walton, Samuel Moore	1918 - 1992	5
12	Ward, William Arthur	1921 - 1994	6
135	Washington, George	1732 - 1799	1
15	Wayne, John	1907 - 1979	4
96	Wells, H. G.	1866- 1946	4
87	West, Mae	1893 - 1980	8
16	Wetmore, Orville C.	1919 -	1
37	Wheatly, Meg	?	2
61	White, Huge	1773 - 1840	1
88	Whitehorn, Katherine	?	1
69	Wilde, Oscar	1854 - 1900	15
127	Wilde, Oscar	1854 - 1900	2
118	Wilde, Stuart	1946 -	4

127	Will, George	1941 -	1
31	Williams, Tennessee	1911 - 1983	1
33	Williamson, Marianne	1952 -	1
83	Willis, Zelda	1960 Est	1
137	Wilson, Woodrow	1856 -1924	1
67	Winfrey, Oprah	1954 -	2
93	Wiseman, Richard	1952 - 2006	5
147	Wojcinski, Alice Barrow	1926 -	2
55	Worden, Don	?	1
55	Worhol, Andy	1928 - 1987	1
55	Wrigley, William Jr.	1861 - 1932	1
97	Yeats, William Butler	1865 -1939	1
35	Zaharis, Nick	1921 -	1
70	Zaharis, Nick	1921 -	3
22	Ziglar, Zig	1926 -	3

About the Author

The author's life experiences started off as a member of the Greatest Generation as defined by Tom Brokaw. To qualify for this dubious honor one had to have experienced the rather primitive living conditions that existed during the Great Depression of the 1930's. Following that, the greatest generation had to win World War 2 in the early 1940's. The author was a B-17 heavy bomber pilot with the Mighty Eighth Air Force stationed in England. His crew-of-nine was shot down on their 31st mission over Natzi Germany and were prisoners of war for the duration. He returned to the University of Florida and the Kappa Sigma Fraternity where he was before being called up for active duty. He graduated with a Bus Ad degree with a major in marketing.

The author's working career was with a large corporation in Delaware as a professional marketing research specialist. He was in charge of conducting industry and consumer surveys and making written and oral reports on the findings .He retired to Palm Coast on the northeast coast of Florida where he joined a dozen or so local and national clubs. He is a past president of the Palm Coast Computer Club, past membership chairman for the Palm Coast Yacht Club and past Commodore of the Matanzas River Yacht Club. He spends a lot of time playing with his computer trying to figure out how to beat the stock market. His hobbies include stamp and coin collecting, photography, genealogy, fishing, scuba diving and yachting on the Chesapeake Bay and the east coast of Florida. He also is a semi-professional boat and car mechanic. Before and after retiring he twice became addicted to golf and recovered both times. So, after eighty-eight years of learning experiences he is still at it and looking for new ventures.

20716835R00114

Printed in Great Britain
by Amazon